Business Models for Teams

See How Your Organization Really Works
and How Each Person Fits In

by Tim Clark and Bruce Hazen,
in collaboration with
225 contributors from 38 countries

Designed by Keiko Onodera

Business Models for Teams

See How Your Organization Really Works and How Each Person Fits In

Portfolio/Penguin

This Book's Business Model

Altogether, 225 people from 39 nations contributed to the writing, editing, and production of *Business Models for Teams*. Draft chapters were uploaded to an online community, where they were reviewed, discussed, and critiqued over a period of 15 months. We estimate that collectively, this group brought to the book more than 5,000 years of full-time professional experience in business, technology, government, academics, medicine, law, design, and other disciplines. The names of all 225 contributors appear on the following two pages.

We are grateful to our contributors, who confirmed our long-standing faith in distributed intelligence—and in a truly global perspective urgently needed in organizations of all kinds here in the United States. Our contributors live in Australia, Austria, Belgium, Brazil, Canada, Chile, China, Colombia, Cypress, Denmark, Finland, France, Germany, Hungary, India, Ireland, Israel, Italy, Japan, Jordan, Luxembourg, Malaysia, Mexico, the Netherlands, New Zealand, the Philippines, Poland, Portugal, Romania, Singapore, Spain, Sweden, Switzerland, Turkey, the United Kingdom, the United Arab Emirates, the United States, and Vietnam.

We particularly thank the following people, who for more than a year spent hundreds of hours submitting and critiquing text, contributing graphic ideas, and helping us collectively shape the direction, tone, and style of the book: Cheryl Sykes, Bob Fariss, Reiner Walter, Marijn Mulder, Jaime Schettini, Adriano Oliveira, Elia Racamonde, Jutta Hastenrath, Dennis Daems, Birgitte Alstrom, Sophie Brown, Beatriz Gonzalez, Erin Liman, Mary Anne Shew, Daniel Weiss, Cheenu Srinivasan, Danielle Leroy, Mitch Spiegel, Luigi Centenaro, Arnulv Rudland, Frederic Caufrier, Edmund Komar, Renate Bouwman, Mercedes Hoss, Thomas Becker, Nicolas de Vicq, Jose Meijer, Neil McGregor, and Mikko Mannila. Above all, thanks to Alexander Osterwalder and Yves Pigneur for inventing the Business Model Canvas.

If the spirit moves you, join us at BusinessModelsForTeams.com to receive all of the tools featured in this book free of charge. You will discover an online community of more than 12,000 business model enthusiasts from 80 countries, including the 225 contributors listed on the following pages.

Co-creators of *Business Models for Teams*

Aclan Can Okur
Adriana Lobo
Adriano Teles da Costa e Oliveira
AJ Shah
Alaa Qari
Alan Scott
Alexander Schmid
Amina Kemiche
Ammar Taqash
Andrea Frausin
Andrew Kidd
Angelina Arciero
Anja Wickert
Ann Ann Low
Annalie Killian
Ariadna Alvarez Delgado
Aricelis Martinez
Arnulv Rudland
Ayman Sheikh Khaleel
Bart Nieuwenhuis
Beatriz Almudena González Torre
Bernie Maloney
Bert Luppens
Birgitte Alstrøm
Birgitte Roujol
Björn Kijl
Bob Fariss
Brenda Coates
Brian Edgar

Brian Haney
Brigitte Tanguay
Bruce Hazen
Bryan Lubic
Carlos Salum
Caroline Bineau
Caroline Ravelo
Cheenu Srinivasan
Cheryl Rochford
Cheryl Sykes
Chimae Cupschalk
Christine Paquette
Christoph Kopp
Christopher Ashe
Conrado Gaytan de la Cruz
Conrado Schlochauer
Cristian Hofmann
Daniel Huber
Daniel Weiss
Danielle Leroy
Dann Bleeker-Pedersen
David M. Blair
David Hubbard
David Nimmo
Dawn Langley
Deanne Lynagh
Denise Taylor

Dennis McCluskey
Dennis Daems
Derrick Tran
Diana Visconti
Dora Luz González Bañales
Doug Gilbert
Doug Morwood
Eddy de Graaf
Edmund Komar
Eduard Ventosa
Eduardo Campos
Eli Ringer
Elia Racamonde
Elizabeth Cable
Enrico Florentino
Eric Nelson
Erik Alexander Leonavicius
Erin Liman
Ernest Buise
Fabiana Mello
Fabio Carvalho
Fabio Nunes
Fabio Petruzzi
Falk Schmidt
Fernando Sáenz Marrero
Francisco Barragan
Francisco Provete
Franck Demay
Frederic Caufrier

Frederic Theismann
Gabrielle Schaffer
Gary Percy
Geoffroy Seive
Ghani Kolli
Gina Condon
Ginés Haro Pastor
Ginger Grant
Gisela Grunda-Hibaly
Glen B. Wheatley
GP designpartners gmbh
Grace Lanni
Greg Loudoun
Gregory S. Nelson
Guida Figueira
Guido Delver
Hadjira Abdoun
Hans Schriever
Hector Miramontes
Hena Rana
Hillel Nissani
Isabel Chaparro
Isabella Bertelli Cabral dos Santos
Jörn Friedrich Dreyer
Jaime Schettini
Jairo Koda
James Saretta
James Wylie

Jan Kyhnau
Jane Leonard
Jason Porterfield
Jaya Machet
Jean-Pierre Savin
Jean-Yves Reynaud
Jeffrey Krames
Jeroen JT Bosman
Joe Costello
John Carnohan
John J Sauer
Jonas Holm
Jonny Law
Jordi Castells
Jorge Carulla
Jorge Pesca Aldrovandi
Jos Meijer
Juan Felipe Monsalve Diez
Jude Rathburn
Judy Weldon
Julia Schlagenhauf
Julie Ann Wood
Justine Lagiewka
Jutta Hastenrath
Katiana Machado
Keiko Onodera
Koen Cuyckens
Laura Stepp
Lina Clark

Liviu Ionescu
Lourdes Orofino
Lourenço de Pauli Souza
Luc E. Morisset
Luigi Centenaro
Lukas Bratt Lejring
Magali Morier
Magda Stawska
Manuel Grassler
Manuela Gsponer
Marco Mathia
Marco Ossani
Maria Monteiro
Marijn Mulders
Markus Heinen
Marsha Brink Stratic
Martin Gaedke
Martin Schoonhoven
Mary Anne Shew
Mathias Wassen
Mats Pettersson
Mattias Nordin
Megan Lacey
Mercedes Hoss-Weis
Michael Lachapelle
Michael Lang
Michael Ruzzi
Michael Makowski

Michael Bertram
Michelle Blanchard
Miki Imazu
Mikko Mannila
Mitchell Spiegel
Mohamad Khawaja
Nadia Circelli
Natalie Currie
Neil McGregor
Niall Reeve-Daly
Nicolas Burkhardt
Nicolas de Vicq
Nige Austin
Olivier Gemoets
Oscar Galvez Tabac
Pallavi Bhadkamkar
Paola Valeri
Paula Quaiser
Paulo Melo
Pedro Fernandez
Peter Cederqvist
Peter Dickinson
Peter Gaunt
Philip Blake
Pierre Chaillou
Rainer Bareiss
Ralf Meyer
Randi Millard

Raymond Guyot
Reiner Walter
Renate Bouwman
Renato Nobre
Rex Foster
Riccardo Donelli
Richard Bell
Roberto Salvato
Robin Lommers
Sara Vilanova
Scott Doniger
Sophie Brown
Stefaan Dumez
Stefan Kappaun
Stephan List
Stuart Lewis
Susanne Zajitschek
Thomas Becker
Thomas Kristiansen
Thomas Fisker Nielsen
Till Leon Kraemer
Tim Clark
Tufan Karaca
Van Le
Verneri Aberg
Victor Gamboa
Viknapergash Guraiah
Vincenzo Baraniello

Origins of the Business Model Canvas

Few people were more surprised than I was when *Business Model Generation* turned into an international bestseller. According to one ranking, it is now the twenty-ninth best-selling management book of all time! The success of that book is based on the Business Model Canvas. Few people know the origins of the Canvas, so Tim and Bruce suggested I share that story here.

I serve as a professor at the University of Lausanne. In the late 1990s teams of graduate students started asking me for advice on new venture ideas and business plans. Many of these were of the "dotcom" variety and involved things like selling craft beers online.

My approach to advising these would-be entrepreneurs was to ask them questions regarding the logic underpinning their proposed ventures. I tried to get them to explain in plain language how their businesses would work—to articulate their business models. I repeated this process with many teams, and over time the questions I posed seemed to naturally fall into nine distinct categories.

When this happened, it occurred to me that perhaps all business models share nine core elements. I did not act on this idea immediately. But it stuck in the back of my mind—and it came roaring back when I agreed to supervise business model–related doctoral studies for a young entrepreneur named Alexander Osterwalder, now founder and CEO of Strategyzer.

For more than a decade, Alex and I worked together to develop, test, and publish our work on business models. During this time, we created a visual, nine-block tool—the Business Model Canvas—that reflected those original nine distinct question categories, though much refined and tested.

The Canvas became the foundation for our co-authored book *Business Model Generation.* In addition to a co-creator community, Alex and I were supported by three colleagues who worked directly on the manuscript: designer Alan Smith, production manager Patrick van der Pijl, and editor Tim Clark.

Tim went on to author *Business Model You,* which applied the Canvas to individual career development for what he calls "personal" business models. Now, Tim and Bruce Hazen have applied the Canvas to internal organizational groups in the book you are now holding: *Business Models for Teams.*

Three things strike me about *Business Models for Teams.*

First, it focuses on using the Canvas to improve an organization's internal operations. This contrasts with the traditional, market-facing use of the Canvas as a strategy-making or strategy-revising tool.

Second, it points out a fast-track way for leaders to boost their effectiveness (rather than their efficiency). Five decades of training, research, and practice have failed to significantly improve organizational leadership, perhaps due to an excessive focus on training team leaders over team members. *Business Models for Teams* offers leaders a way to share operational ownership and show everyone how they fit into the workplace.

Third, *Business Models for Teams* shows how the same tool can be used to create understanding and clarity at organizational, team, and individual levels. Along the way, it in-troduces several useful new tools and techniques that will benefit anyone who serves others as a leader, manager, or mentor.

Who better than Tim Clark and Bruce Hazen to write this practical and inspiring handbook on bridging the gap between *me* and *we*? Based on instructive cases and stories, Tim and Bruce propose to "move beyond words and pinpoint problems with how individuals, teams, and organizations work."

Dear readers, let yourselves be charmed by this practical handbook. Throughout each chapter, Tim and Bruce pass on their approach with passion and clear examples. We are convinced you will discover new tools and techniques to become *me*-to-*we* practitioners.

Yves Pigneur

professor of management information sciences, University of Lausanne, Switzerland; co-author (with Alexander Osterwalder) of *Business Model Generation*

People Like You Featured in this Book

Contents

I. A Bigger Theory of Work

See new ways to lead and better ways to work.

II. Business Models

Learn to use a powerful tool for describing and analyzing organizational, team, and personal business models.

III. Teamwork

Boost teamwork with new tools that complement business model thinking.

IV. Application Guide

Discover how others did it, and how to make it work for yourself, your team, and your organization.

Section I

A Bigger Theory of Work

See new ways to lead and better ways to work.

Chapter 1

From *Me* to *We*

The Player-Coach

"I noticed you don't have enough players. Can I join your team?"

He looked hopeful. And in his international soccer jersey, he also looked knowledgeable, something the rest of us could not claim. Our motley team of graduate students took to the field each week to compete in California's San Jose Industrial Soccer League, originally so we could enjoy the excellent post-game parties. We were tied for last place.

"Why not?" our captain replied. "We need all the help we can get."

"That you do!" the visitor said. Everyone laughed.

The visitor introduced himself as Ramy. He had been a player-coach in Egypt for years before coming to the United States for graduate school. His appearance was timely: we had recently tired of playing poorly, of spending time and energy on soccer without showing much improvement. Ramy joined us and agreed to serve as player-coach.

Things changed. Ramy started bringing out the best in everyone by teaching what he called "a bigger theory of the game." And over time, we slowly transformed into a real team. The differences between our old and new styles of play were dramatic:

- Most of us were simply *chasing the ball*. Ramy taught us to see and relate *to each other*.

- Ramy taught us to strive to be the best *playmakers* rather than the best *players*.

- We had focused excessively on playing *positions*. Ramy taught us to *see what was happening on the entire field*.

- We had been playing mainly to socialize. Ramy gave us a bigger purpose: *improving our skills and becoming a winning team*.

One season after our new player-coach joined us, we placed second in our league. Spouses and friends turned into enthusiastic supporters. And we still loved the post-game parties, especially because we could now celebrate our wins.[1]

From *Me* to *We*

Ramy helped transform a group of amateur U.S. soccer players into a true team. How? By appealing to four things that motivate people:

Purpose
People want to be part of something greater than themselves. Ramy brought a greater purpose: becoming a winning team.

Autonomy
People want to direct their own lives. Ramy showed teammates how to make things happen.

Relatedness
People want to feel connected. Ramy taught his teammates to work together and make plays.

Mastery
People want to get better and better at something. Ramy showed his teammates how to build their skills.[2]

Though Ramy was teaching soccer, he might just as well have been tackling a challenge faced by many organizations: coaching people to stop focusing on *me* and start focusing on *we*. In short, building better teams.

Every leader wants better teamwork. Yet all teams are, to some extent, conflicted and dysfunctional. Teamwork consultant Patrick Lencioni says this happens for the simple reason that teams "are made up of imperfect human beings" facing a constant, internal tug-of-war.[3]

At work, people struggle to balance personal needs (*What's in it for me?*) with team aims (*What's best for the group?*). Personal career decisions, too, often seem like tough choices between survival and seeking meaningful work. This tension between *me* and *we* is biological, permanent, and irresolvable, says Pulitzer Prize-winning Harvard biologist Edward O. Wilson:

> *Are we built to pledge our lives to a group? Or to place ourselves and our families above all else? Scientific evidence . . . suggests that we are both of these things simultaneously . . . The products of the two opposing vectors . . . are hardwired in our emotions and reasoning, and cannot be erased.*[4]

No wonder leading a team is so challenging; it demands tirelessly moving back and forth between personal needs and group goals.

Leaders must somehow address both the self-serving *me* and the group-serving *we*. But the *me-we* conflict is inevitable, so eliminating it is impossible. Instead, a good team-builder uses this tension to everyone's benefit. The goal is to shift people toward *we* behavior by artfully recognizing everyone's *me*. *Business Models for Teams* will show you how—and like Ramy, make you a standout player-coach for *your* organization.

How Does *Me-to-We* Work?

The *me-to-we* approach works by adopting a Bigger Theory of Work. Just as Ramy steered his teammates away from playing "positions," the Bigger Theory defines work not in terms of *jobs* but in terms of *roles*.

Job descriptions define duties, tasks, and expected outcomes. In contrast, role descriptions focus on relationships to other people, much as Ramy taught unskilled soccer players to work together rather than merely chase the ball. For example, on a project team, Kevin could be given the role of communications director. "Communications director" is not a job title, it is a *role* Kevin will play in communicating his team's actions to the rest of the organization.

The Business Model Canvas

The Bigger Theory of Work also sees work not in terms of *organizational structure* but rather in terms of *business models*. Organization charts describe reporting relationships within an enterprise. But they tell us little about how an organization works as a system.

Business models, on the other hand, describe what an organizational system actually does, for whom, and how its elements are related. A business model shows a system "happening all at once"—much as Ramy showed players how to see the entire game unfolding on a soccer field. Starting in the next chapter, you will learn to use the Business Model Canvas, a powerful tool for depicting and understanding business models.

The Business Model Canvas can be used to create a "systems view" of organizations at three levels: enterprise, team, and individual. An *enterprise business model* shows how an entire organization creates and delivers value to customers outside the organization. A *team business model* shows how a group creates and delivers value, often to "customers" inside the organization. A *personal business model* shows how an individual creates and delivers value.

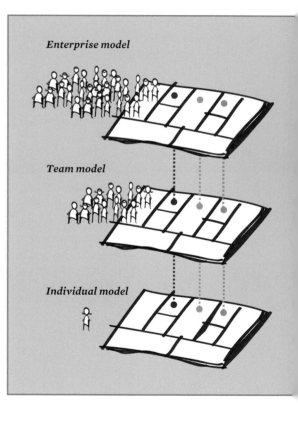

Enterprise model

Team model

Individual model

Who This Book is for and Why

Think of the three levels as a stacked tier with the enterprise model on top. Viewing an organization this way reveals workplace interdependencies and begins imparting a sense of relatedness to people who may be accustomed to thinking of work in terms of proscribed "jobs" that rarely transcend group or functional boundaries. This is where people begin discovering how an organization really works—and how they fit in.

Business Models For Teams is for anyone who oversees other people, and who, like Ramy, want to strengthen their teams—and stay in the game! The methods described can be used in most organizations, whether non-profit or for-profit.

Good teamwork means more than cooperation and communication. It means people are both self-directed and working on important things, not merely keeping busy. So a key goal of the book is to teach you specific ways you can help people become more self-directed, and, as Warren Buffett famously said, help you "lead more and manage less."

Leadership Basics

You can benefit from the methods and techniques described regardless of your background or experience. But basic management or supervisory skills will be important if you plan to use the book to teach or train others.

Business Models For Teams is not about leadership basics, and it does not recommend one particular style of leadership. But if you feel a need to revisit the fundamentals, one enduring model that has informed generations of front-line managers and executives is situational leadership, originally introduced by Paul Hersey and Ken Blanchard.[5]

Situational leadership says that leaders cannot rely on a single behavioral mode or single lens through which to view people and their needs. Rather, they must adapt their style to fit different people and different situations. A popular adaptation of the situational leadership model is presented in the bestseller *The One Minute Manager*.[6]

The best way for most people to grow as a leader is to improve basic management skills: things like building trust, delivering feedback, and giving recognition and acknowledgment.[7] See the bibliography on page 250 for suggested readings on leadership and related topics.

"Accidental" Leadership and Three Thinking Styles

People often become leaders "by accident." That is, they are promoted to leadership positions mainly because of strong technical or functional competence, not necessarily because they exhibited strong management or supervisory skills. As a result, many new leaders must literally learn to think differently.

Here is why. When people begin their careers they are "testing their training"—they seek direction and depend on others to teach them new or better ways of working. This career stage is characterized by **dependent** thinking.

Once people develop a specialty and a reputation for competence, they tend to trust their own experience and become more self-directed. This career stage is characterized by **independent** thinking.

But when people start leading others, they must think about systems and about relationships— relationships between people and between groups of people. This requires **interdependent** or systems thinking. The most practical, readily-understandable way to grasp systems and inter-dependencies is to graphically depict them with business models.[8]

Improving your facility with business models will help you tremendously as a leader. It will also help you differentiate between the three thinking styles (dependent, independent, and interdependent/systems), sharpen your ability to recognize the three styles in others, and help coworkers learn and practice the appropriate style.

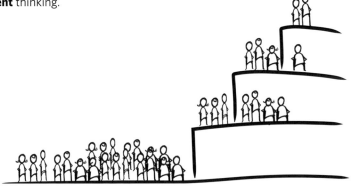

Why *Business Models for Teams?*

Business models are ordinarily used to better serve *external* Customers. This is *strategy*: the logic of creating and delivering benefits to markets. In most organizations, only executives work on strategy.

Rather than strategy, we focus on using business models to better serve *internal* Customers. This is *operations*. Operations is where most people work.

Business Model Generation defined a new way to describe organizational strategy. *Business Model You* applied the method to individuals. Now *Business Models for Teams* shows strategy and operations together—so people understand what to do at work each day.

When Words Are Not Enough—or Too Much

Newly-promoted leaders who read leadership books or take leadership training often come away with a fresh vocabulary that describes skillful leading. Yet they may still lack the capacity to demonstrate leadership or develop it in others, and instead rely on leader-like pronouncements made under two mistaken assumptions:

1. Everyone understands my words the way I understand and intend them.

2. Everyone will now take appropriate action, based on my words.

There is nothing wrong with words, of course. But words alone cannot handle the task of explaining or understanding a complex, multi-dimensional system such as an organization. To understand a system, leaders need physical tools (third objects[9]) that allow people to see an entire system at once. Third objects such as Canvases, LEGO® bricks, sticky notes, flip charts, and drawings efficiently symbolize or model relationships too complex for words.

Third object tools gently guide users away from the abstract world of discussion and toward the concrete world of construction.[10] Active construction uncovers tacit knowledge, empowers less verbal people, and makes it easier for everyone to articulate and share thoughts with colleagues. Third objects also reduce conflict by focusing people on the work that needs to be done, and reducing the effects of personality, politics, and the tendency for groups to adopt the opinions of the most articulate speaker. What is more, they are highly engaging and inspire people to change their behavior.

Experienced me-to-we practitioners find third object tools indispensable, so you will find plenty of examples throughout this book. These tools will help you move beyond words and pinpoint problems with how individuals, teams, and organizations work.

An organization expressed using LEGO® bricks

Clarifying Your Role

But what follows that—helping people fit into organizations and become productive—demands solid leadership skills. Inexperienced leaders will struggle to accomplish this crucial goal. If you use the tools in this book to uncover problems, be sure you and your team have the capacity and commitment to address them.

New leaders tend to over-focus on matching their behavior to the job they have just been hired to do. But they rarely explain their leadership role to those they supervise. As a result, few subordinates understand the new leader's role. Rather, they infer it based on isolated interactions with that leader. If you want colleagues to better support you ("manage up" from their perspective), do not leave them guessing; give them a full description of your leadership role.

Roles—especially leaders' roles—are bound to change over time. So it is essential to openly and explicitly review peoples' roles, including your own leadership role. Avoid lecturing, talking down to direct reports, or reviewing job descriptions. Simply describe your respective roles. If you want a team to move toward more distributed decision-making and self-directed action, for example, you might explain that your role will shift from that of an answer-giver who solves problems to that of a questioner who helps others frame problems.

The Approach: A Quick Overview

You will start learning specific methods for boosting teamwork in the next chapter. The methods can be used in many combinations, but here is a quick overview of one typical approach:

1. Participants draw personal business models

Individual team members use the Personal Business Model Canvas to depict what they currently do at work—and what they would like to do in the future. This causes participants to think beyond activities and recognize who they help at work—the first step toward acknowledging the crucial workplace interdependencies that underpin good cooperation. The process of creating "as-is" and "to-be" models and sharing the resulting insights prompts participants to become more communicative and aware of gaps in their own ability to contribute. These are solid steps toward better teamwork.

2. Participants define their team model

Next, using the same Canvas tool, team members collectively model the work they do as a group. This is usually an eye-opener; it visually clarifies the team's purpose and causes participants to recognize other groups they help at work, thus acknowledging enterprise-level connections. This triggers awareness of both the team and the enterprise as dynamic, feedback-dependent systems rather than static "mechanisms." Again, the process of creating the model and sharing collective insights helps participants develop more situational awareness, a big step toward better teamwork and self-directed action.

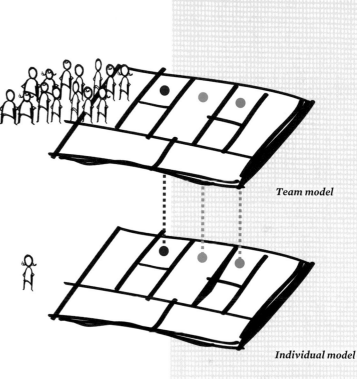

Team model

Individual model

3. Participants map individual contributions onto their team model

Participants "map" their individual contributions onto the team model, pinpointing where they create or add value to what the team does. This brings inefficiencies and opportunities into sharp relief, and often reveals important work that needs doing. In turn, this creates compelling opportunities for participants to commit to new tasks or roles in front of their colleagues. Meanwhile, both the content and the process of the exercise reinforce cooperation and communication.

People who experience this process report breakthroughs in thinking, awareness, and most important, behavior. You will meet a number of them later in the book, and learn how they used the approach to overcome tough problems and pursue intriguing opportunities. You will learn how to use the tools, and how to facilitate the process with your own team.

In the meantime, you can be confident knowing that the Business Model Canvas has been extensively tested by both for-profit and non-profit organizations for more than a decade. It has been downloaded more than five million times and is being used by tens of thousands of top-notch enterprises worldwide.[11]

Defining Your Team's *Why*

Many organizations use mission or purpose statements to tell the world *what they do and why*. At their best, these statements describe an inspiring, memorable purpose that guides the organization and its workers. At their worst, they leave readers confused.

Most such statements fall somewhere between the two extremes. Consider the text at right (as of this writing still in use by a century-old, billion-dollar company).

We are strongly committed to our customers.
Our ambition is to provide meaningful benefits to all our customers.
We listen closely and align our activities to their needs.
Our goal is the improvement of their overall quality of life, and being a trustworthy and reliable partner in their well-being.

This statement means well but is bafflingly vague. What does this company do? Is it a service provider or product manufacturer? Does it grow food? Manufacture bowling balls? Offer retirement planning services? Who are its customers? Why does it exist?

Many organizations fail to use simple, clear language to share their *why*. The company in this example has been doing wonderful things for humanity for more than a century. Why not tell the world in easily understandable language, such as:

> *Ease the suffering of the sick and injured by developing powerful, safe, pain-relieving drugs.*

You may not be in a position to rewrite an organization's *why* statement (though that is a terrific exercise to try). But you are probably in a position to restate the purpose of a team you lead—preferably in collaboration with your team members. Here are some tips:

1. Keep it Short and Memorable

The example on the facing page is 49 words long and entirely forgettable. The revised version above is 14 words long and easy to remember. *Why* statements are useful only if people remember them.

2. Communicate Both Why and What

The first example communicates nothing about what the company does—or why. The revised version communicates precisely what the company does, and this makes the *why* obvious.

3. State the Higher Purpose

The first example lacks a purpose beyond being "committed to customers." In contrast, the revised version leads with the higher purpose of "ease suffering."

4. Write in Third Person

The first example is written in first person: Every sentence starts with either "we" or "our." But a *why* statement is not about your team—it is about what your team does for others. Write it in the third person (anything other than *I, we,* or *you*).

To sum up: Meaningful *why* statements avoid jargon and ambiguous language. They concisely tell the world what a team does and why it is important. They articulate a higher purpose and are other-serving rather than self-serving. *Why* statements are meaningful, of course, only if organizations stay true to them.

THE PRICE OF PURPOSE: $2 BILLION

Helena Foukes faced the most important decision of her career—and the most profound question her employer had ever asked itself.

Foukes's employer, U.S. pharmacy giant CVS, was grappling with a dilemma: Could it continue, in good conscience, to sell cigarettes alongside health aids and medicines?

It was no trivial decision. Tobacco-related sales accounted for $2 billion of CVS revenues each year.

Ultimately, though, Foukes and her team decided to affirm CVS's purpose and remove all tobacco and tobacco-related products from store shelves.

"That decision really became a symbol both internally and externally," says Foukes. "We're a health-care company."

Why CVS Quit Smoking, The New York Times July 12, 2015

Things to Try on Monday Morning

To help you start teambuilding, each chapter in this book ends with
Things to Try on Monday Morning, exercises you can try immediately.
The first one appears on the facing page.

Draft Your Team's Why Statement

Draft your own team's *why* statement in the box below. Keep it short—15 words or fewer is a good rule of thumb. Recall guidelines from the previous pages: *1. Keep it Short and Memorable, 2. Communicate the What and Why, 3. State the Higher Purpose, 4. Write in Third Person*

Alternative Exercise: Write your organization's mission or purpose statement in the box below. How does it measure up against the guidelines? If the highest-ranking executive in your organization asked you to create a new mission or purpose statement, what would you write?

You Can Do it!

Even as this book traveled from the printer to seller warehouses, some of the business models described within it have changed. Organizations have shifted, teams have morphed, and people have transitioned into different roles—or moved on to different organizations. Whether at the organizational, team, or personal level, business models constantly change—as they must.

That is why this book focuses on teaching you the *process* of modeling, rather than encouraging you to pursue the "perfect" model for your team or organization.

The good news is that your growing ability to recognize, describe, analyze, and innovate with business models will make you an even better team leader and drive greater personal and team success.

Using business models means discussing an organization's purpose and strategy. That can be daunting, especially if you work in a larger enterprise.

But fear not! Start from where you stand. You can experiment with business models without petitioning other leaders for buy-in or disrupting long-standing processes. The truth is that almost any leader—regardless of number of people led—can dramatically boost teamwork and self-direction at work *right now*. Read on to learn how.

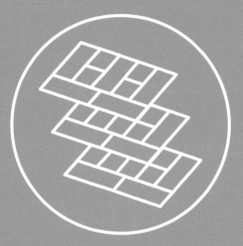

Section II

Business Models

Learn to use a powerful tool for describing and analyzing organizational, team, and personal business models.

Chapter 2

Modeling Organizations

Tweak in Logic Sparks Revolution

Photograph courtesy of Xerox Corporation

The Haloid Photographic Company, founded in Rochester, New York more than a century ago, is a largely forgotten firm. But at a pivotal moment in Haloid's history, a simple business model tweak utterly transformed the company into a global technology powerhouse, sparking an information-sharing revolution and creating an iconic brand still recognized everywhere today.

In 1958, Haloid had invented a plain-paper photocopier it believed could revolutionize how information was shared in large and medium-sized enterprises that relied on carbon paper or special coated-paper machines for making copies. But Haloid's device, dubbed the Model 914, was expensive and as big as a deep freezer, weighing 648 pounds (nearly 300 kilograms). IBM, one of Haloid's potential manufacturing partners for the 914, hired the distinguished consultancy Arthur D. Little to investigate the device's market potential. In their conclusion, the consultants wrote, "Model 914 has no future in the office copying market."[1]

A second study conducted by consultancy Ernst & Ernst produced only slightly less pessimistic findings. But Haloid persisted, confident its machine could unlock tremendous value for far-sighted customers.

Soon afterward, it occurred to product planning chief John Glavin that Haloid could change how the company offered the machine. Instead of asking customers to purchase the expensive device outright, why not offer a low-cost lease, put a meter on the machine, and charge users a per-copy fee? This would dramatically lower the initial cash investment and give customers a chance to assess the machine's usefulness. Haloid management decided to try this approach.

Aside from the switch to metered leasing, nothing else changed: the device remained exactly the same, as did Haloid's customers. Yet this simple tweak in benefit delivery logic revolutionized the industry. Within a dozen years, Haloid's sales skyrocketed from U.S. $30 million to U.S. $1.2 billion.[2] Along the way, the company adopted a new name: Xerox.

The new photocopier created tremendous benefits for enterprises: it enabled them to replicate and share important information quickly and at low cost (remember, this was before the invention of personal computers and the Internet).

Customers embraced the amazing device and made billions of copies, matched by billions of dollars in sales. The new business model, whereby Xerox leased photocopier hardware at low cost and charged customers for actual copies made each month, worked brilliantly for decades.

A Fading Model

But trouble loomed. Japanese makers released smaller, highly-competitive copiers. In the early 1990s, commercial Internet access services became available, and in 1993, Adobe Systems made its PDF file specifications publicly available free of charge. Slowly, digital files and the Internet began to replace paper

as the preferred way to replicate and share information. Xerox's traditional copier-leasing business model began to show its age.

Meanwhile, Xerox aggressively embraced the digital revolution, inventing or developing transformational technologies such as the personal computer, the laser printer, the computer mouse, the graphical user interface, and Ethernet.[3] Yet it was unable to commercialize these important technologies. Instead, they were exploited by other companies—notably Apple Computer—that used business models very different from Xerox's copier-leasing logic.

In years following, Xerox was buffeted by waves of technical, social, and economic change. The paperless office, the "green" revolution, and cost-cutting demanded by harder economic times steadily undermined its mainstay photocopier business model.[4] Though Xerox remains an international technology powerhouse, as of this writing its market capitalization is

less than one-fiftieth that of Apple Computer, a key beneficiary of Xerox innovations.[5]

Xerox's extraordinary history teaches two lessons. First, it is possible for an enterprise to literally transform itself by altering its business model. Second, even brilliant business models eventually expire. In industry after industry, business model lifespans are shrinking as technological, economic, and social change accelerates—and competition intensifies.

Amid this turbulence, business modeling skills are essential for leaders and aspiring leaders alike. Enter the Business Model Canvas: an extraordinarily useful tool that depicts the logic by which enterprises create and deliver value to customers, and are compensated for doing so.

Business models are crucial to organizations. But how are they described? How do you express them in a usable way?

The Business Model Canvas is a useful tool for doing just those things.

The Canvas is a single sheet of paper printed with nine different rectangular blocks.

Think of the Canvas as a relationship map depicting nine logically-linked elements: elements common to most enterprises. Each rectangular element is called a building block. Each building block describes people, places, things, intangible assets, or actions needed for the enterprise to run effectively.

Viewing all nine building blocks as one cohesive whole helps people 1) understand the organization's purpose, and 2) see crucial organizational interdependencies they might otherwise fail to recognize.

Together the nine building blocks describe a business model: the logic by which an enterprise creates and delivers benefits to customers—and is compensated for doing so.[6]

The Business Model Canvas

Key Partners

People or organizations that perform Key Activities or provide Key Resources to the enterprise.

Key Activities

Actions needed to create, communicate, sell, or deliver Value Propositions to Customers.

Value Propositions

Benefits (solutions or satisfactions) delivered via services or products.

Customer Relationships

Post-sale communications to ensure Customer satisfaction and offer additional benefits.

Customer Segments

One or more distinct groups that benefit from Value Propositions, whether purchased or not.

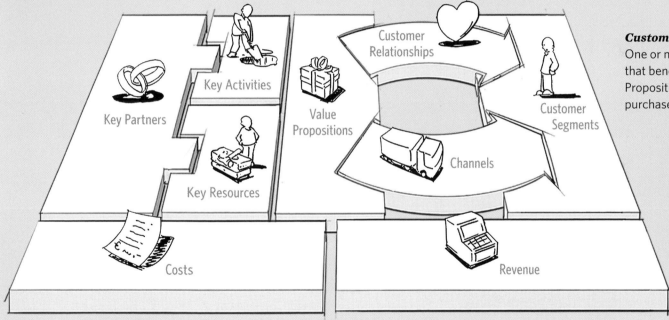

Costs

Expenses incurred acquiring Key Resources, performing Key Activities, or working with Key Partners.

Key Resources

People, property, money, or intangibles essential for creating and delivering Value Propositions to Customers.

Channels

The touchpoints by which the enterprise communicates, sells, and delivers Value Propositions.

Revenue

Funds received when Customers pay for Value Propositions.

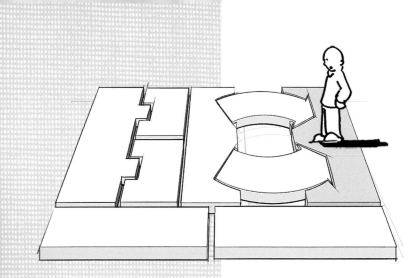

Customer Segments

Customers are the reason enterprises exist. All organizations—whether in the for-profit, non-profit, social, government, legal, or medical fields—serve one or more distinct Customer groups. Some organizations prefer the term *client* or *stakeholder* to Customer.

Some enterprises serve both paying and non-paying Customers. Most Google users, for example, pay Google nothing for its services. Yet without millions of non-paying Customers, Google would have nothing to sell to advertisers. So non-paying Customers may be essential to a business model's success.

Sometimes Customers actually cost the enterprise money. Governments and hospitals, for example, may be obligated to provide costly services to Customers who are unable to pay.

Key Points About Customers
- Different Customer groups require different Value Propositions, and may require different Channels or Customer Relationships
- An enterprise may have paying, non-paying, or cost-inducing Customers
- Enterprises often earn far more from one Customer group than from another
- External Customers reside outside the organization. Internal Customers reside in the same organization.

Value Propositions

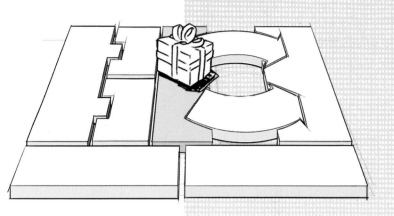

Think of Value Propositions as bundles of services or products that create benefits (value) for Customers. The ability to deliver better value is the main reason why Customers select one enterprise over another.

Value Propositions can provide different types of benefits:

Functional
Functional benefits mean the Value Proposition accomplishes a specific task. For example, offering temporary personnel services helps Customers avoid the high cost and legal obligations incurred by hiring full-time employees.

Social
Social benefits mean the Value Proposition improves how Customers are perceived by others. For example, a car buyer might select a Mercedes-Benz to signify success and good taste.

Emotional
Emotional benefits mean the Value Proposition helps Customers feel a certain way. For example, people may buy cosmetics or clothes to feel attractive, younger, or more desirable.

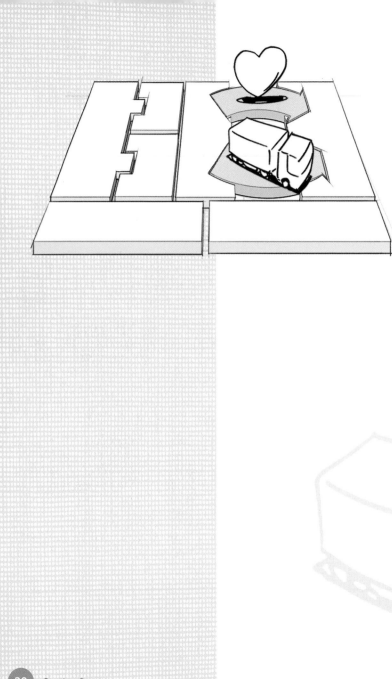

Channels and Customer Relationships

Together, Channels and Customer Relationships comprise the five-phase marketing process by which an enterprise communicates, sells, and delivers its Value Propositions, then follows up to make sure Customers are satisfied—and to propose additional benefits.

Think of Channels as touchpoints or pathways by which the enterprise 1) creates Awareness, 2) induces Evaluation, 3) enables Purchase, and 4) executes Delivery. These four steps attract prospective buyers and convert them to Customers.

Think of Customer Relationships as what happens *after* prospects are converted to Customers. In this final phase of the five-phase marketing process, the enterprise provides post-sales support and offers Customers additional benefits in the form of other Value Propositions.[7]

Note: Most enterprises use the same Channel touchpoints for both new and existing Customers.

The Five-Phase Marketing Process

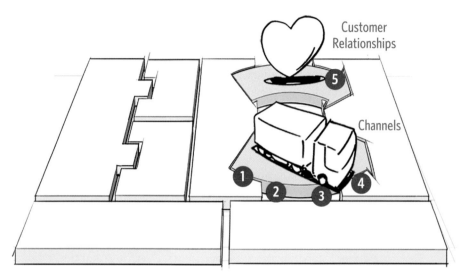

Customer Relationships

Channels

5 Followup

Touchpoints
In-person, telephone, chat, e-mail, teleconference, Web, wiki, mail-in warranty or response, co-creation, etc.

Actions
Ask Customers about their experience, resolve problems, deal with claims, co-develop services or products, introduce additional Value Propositions

4 Delivery

Touchpoints
On-site/off-site acceptance (service) or pickup (product), parcel delivery service, digital transfer, online activation, etc.

Actions
Perform service in-person or off-site, ship or transfer goods, transfer files or activate account, etc.

1 Awareness

Touchpoints
In-person, online, signage, trade shows, videos, direct mail, word-of-mouth, press conferences, print, television, radio, etc.

Actions
Educate, inform, alert, promote, advertise

2 Evaluation

Touchpoints
In-person or online demonstration, trial, or interview, mailed or digital sample, etc.

Actions
Present, offer trial or sample, test, share testimonials

3 Purchase

Touchpoints
Online, on-site, in-person, call center, etc.

Actions
Offer payment methods and terms preferred by Customers: cash, debit/credit, electronic, bank transfer, etc.

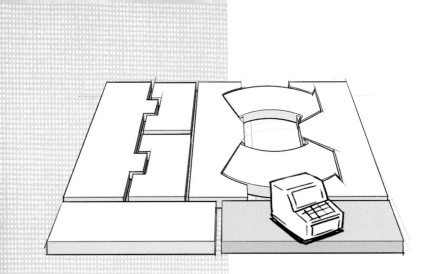

Revenue

These are funds the enterprise receives when Customers purchase services or products and are satisfied (they do not claim refunds). Customer payment preferences signal the actual value for which Customers are willing to pay.

Remember Haloid? Its business exploded after it made lease payments (monthly fee plus per-copy charge) available in its Revenue building block. Customers were unwilling to pay a high price to own an expensive asset (a product) but they were happy to pay smaller, ongoing fees for the ability to replicate and share information as needed (a service).

Payments can take many forms:

- *Asset sale*
- *Lease or rental fee*
- *Subscription charge*
- *Licensing fee*
- *Brokerage fee*
- *Placement or advertising fee*
- *Auction-based dynamic pricing*

Be sure to differentiate between payment *form* (lease vs. outright purchase) and payment *method* (credit card vs. PayPal). Sometimes changing a payment method can have a big effect on Revenue, too.

Key Resources

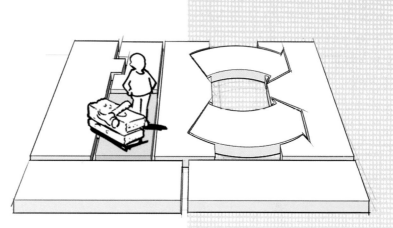

When listing Key Resources, include only those assets truly essential for creating, communicating, selling, and delivering Value Propositions. Ignore secondary assets commonly used by most enterprises, such as desks or computers.

Enterprises use the following four types of resources:

People
Skilled and unskilled workers, including employees, contractors, temporary hires, and specialized service providers

Tangible Property
Vehicles, computers, buildings, land, equipment, furniture, tools, supplies

Intangible Property
Brands, methods, systems, software, patents, copyrights, licenses

Money
Cash, stock, receivables, lines of credit, financial guarantees

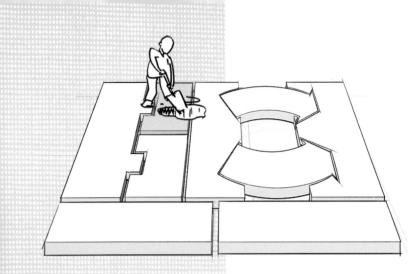

Key Activities

These are the important things an organization must do to make its business model work, specifically creating, communicating, selling, and delivering Value Propositions—then following up to ensure Customer satisfaction. You might find it helpful to think of three types of Key Activities:

Make
This includes designing, developing, manufacturing, problem-solving, or delivering services or products (services are "consumed" as they are delivered).

Sell
This includes advocating, demonstrating, promoting, or advertising specific services or products (or the enterprise itself).

Support
This means activities not directly associated with either making or selling. Examples could include supervising, accounting, or maintaining computer networks.

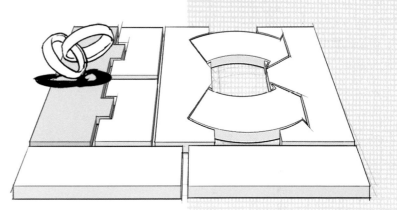

Key Partners

Many enterprises find it too expensive or inefficient to own all Key Resources or perform every Key Activity themselves. So they find partners who can provide help or resources essential to making the business model work.

Note: Key Partners may differ from suppliers. Suppliers often compete with each other to win the enterprise as a Customer, and they can be readily replaced. Key Partners, on the other hand, are not easily found or replaced. The enterprise may have to compete with other enterprises to acquire a Key Partner.

Sometimes, though, suppliers *are* Key Partners. Apple's relationship with Foxconn may be one example.

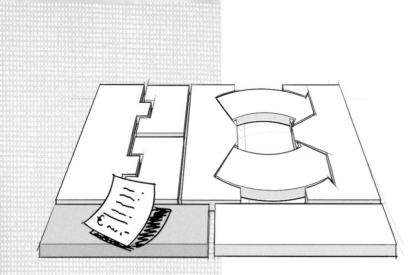

Costs

These are expenses incurred in acquiring Key Resources, performing Key Activities, or engaging Key Partners. The ongoing expense of operating under a particular business model can be roughly calculated after defining elements in these three building blocks.[8]

A business model is sustainable only if Revenues consistently exceed (or at least equal) Costs. Subtract Costs from Revenues to calculate what an enterprise earns.

Costs may be:

- Fixed: salaries, leases
- Variable: cost of goods or services, contingent labor
- Non-cash: amortization, goodwill, externalities

Together the nine building blocks describe a business model, which can be depicted using the Business Model Canvas.[9]

The Business Model Canvas is provided by the makers of *Business Models Generation* and Strategyzer under a Creative Commons license.

Haloid's Photocopier Business Model

The Canvas on the facing page describes Haloid's business model at a very high level. Have a look, then refer to the notes below.

Customers

Office operations of corporations, government offices, medical facilities, and other large and mid-sized enterprises comprised the customer base.

Value Proposition

Haloid enabled easy, low-cost information sharing. "Value" means benefits to Customers, and *benefits are often intangible.* In this case, benefits were best created by leasing the product rather than by selling it outright.

Channels and Customer Relationships

Copiers installed on-site served as the Channel's delivery mechanism. Customer Relationships were handled by maintenance technicians and salespeople visiting Customer sites to confirm satisfaction or diagnose and fix problems.

Revenue

Revenue was generated by lease payments, per-copy charges, supply fees, and service fees. Preference for lease payments showed that Customers valued service over product ownership.

Key Resources

Haloid's Key Resources included electrophotography ("xerography") patents and related inventions, outstanding technical expertise, a strong reputation, and excellent managers and engineers.

Key Activities

Manufacturing copiers, maintaining copiers, and selling leases were the three most important activities, followed by research and development. Note that collectively, Key Activities create Value, but *they do not constitute Value in and of themselves from a customer's perspective.*

Key Partners

Some patents were supplied by Battelle.

Costs

The main costs were salaries, manufacturing cost of goods, building and equipment leases, and inventory financing.

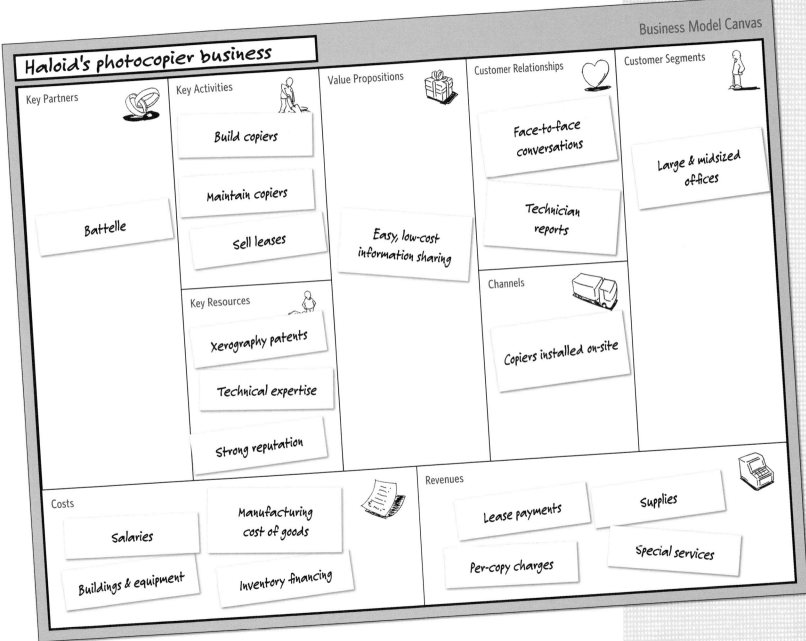

Haloid's photocopier business

Key Partners

Battelle

Key Activities

Build copiers

Maintain copiers

Sell leases

Key Resources

Xerography patents

Technical expertise

Strong reputation

Value Propositions

Easy, low-cost information sharing

Customer Relationships

Face-to-face conversations

Technician reports

Channels

Copiers installed on-site

Customer Segments

Large & midsized offices

Costs

Salaries

Manufacturing cost of goods

Buildings & equipment

Inventory financing

Revenues

Lease payments

Per-copy charges

Supplies

Special services

Using Business Models to Strengthen Teamwork

Business models are essential to organizational strategy: they can make the difference between failure and success. Many books, articles, videos, and courses are available to learn more about business modeling (see pages 250–251).

Traditionally, business modeling has focused on *strategy*: how to create and deliver the best possible benefits to Customers. Benefiting Customers, after all, is an enterprise's main purpose. So it is vital that workers understand that purpose—and Customers' crucial importance. After all, Customers ultimately pay all the bills, including salaries!

But business modeling can help organizations in another, equally important way: *strengthening internal teamwork by showing people why their work matters.*

As an example, consider how Steve Brown's restaurant, Modello, operates. Like most restaurants, Modello can be divided into two parts: the dining area (the "front of the house"), and the kitchen/dishroom (the "back of the house"). The dining area is like the right-hand side of the Canvas: the Customer-facing part. The kitchen/dishroom area is like the left-hand side of the Canvas: the internal operations Customers do not see.

Note that at Modello, as in most organizations, the majority of workers do not deal directly with diners (external Customers). They deal mainly with their colleagues (internal Customers).

The tasks each restaurant worker performs are clear: the dishwasher cleans and replenishes dinnerware and cookware, the servers take orders and bring meals to diners, and so forth. What is important for workers to understand, though, is *how their actions affect Customers*.

A worker's effect on Customers can be depicted with a "teamwork table" showing each person's role, tasks performed, and the positive or negative consequences of task performance. The teamwork table clearly shows everyone *why their work matters.*

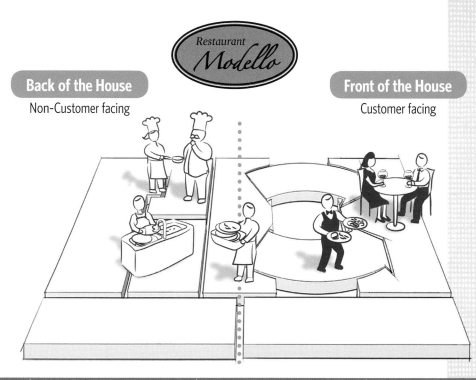

Restaurant
Modello

Back of the House
Non-Customer facing

Front of the House
Customer facing

	Role		Tasks	Result of task success	Consequence of task failure
Customer facing workers	Servers		Take orders correctly and politely, serve meals, deliver checks, collect payments	Positive dining experience, bigger tips	Unsatisfying dining experience, smaller tips, unfavorable social media postings
	Busser		Clear dishes, clean tables and chairs	Guests enjoy clean table settings that enhance dining experience, bigger tips	Guest experience diminished by dirty table setting, smaller tips, unfavorable social media postings
Non-Customer facing workers	Chef		Create excellent menu and ensure its correct execution	Good food, convenience for guests, enjoyment for guests	Disappointing dining experience, loss of Customers, smaller tips, unfavorable social media postings
	Cooks		Correctly and consistently prepare menu items	Predictably positive dining experience, bigger tips	Unpredictable dining experience, loss of Customers, smaller tips, unfavorable social media postings
	Dishwasher		Clean tableware	Impression of cleanliness and good hygiene, bigger tips	Guest experience diminished by unclean tableware, smaller tips, unfavorable social media postings

Developing "Situation Savvy"

In a well-run restaurant like Modello, workers naturally develop good situational awareness (what we call "situation savvy"). Workers physically hand off tasks to one another, so they must cooperate to be effective in their roles. Feedback from fellow workers, diners, managers, and social media is immediate. At Modello, tips are shared equally by all staff, so at the end of each shift everyone learns exactly how diners ranked their performance as a team!

But tips alone tell an incomplete story. No single worker at Modello performs all three Key Activities, so to fully understand their collective performance, staff members discuss—*from their respective viewpoints*—what happened during the shift. This builds situation savvy.

In many organizations, few people have direct contact with Customers. Work product may be digitally passed on to remote colleagues. Customer feedback is delayed for weeks or months, and financial performance is shared quarterly at best. As a result, situation savvy—and strong teamwork—can be tough to build.

To make matters more challenging, when services or products ordered by Customers are complex, tasks must often be broken down to the point that workers fail to grasp the service or product as a whole. People may fail to understand what value their own teams create—or which Customers ultimately benefit from their efforts. So it is hardly surprising that people end up laboring in isolated silos and failing to grasp how and whom they benefit through their work.

Using the Canvas and a teamwork table causes people to locate their work within the overall logic of enterprise operations and see how their day-to-day activities benefit Customers. This leads to better collaboration and more self-directed action. That lets leaders spend more time actually leading instead of problem-solving or mediating conflict.

In later chapters, you will learn specific ways to use the Canvas and other third object tools to strengthen situation savvy in your workplace. This will help people become less dependent on supervisors or managers to solve problems.

Next, consider a crucial but often overlooked element of organizational models: externalities.

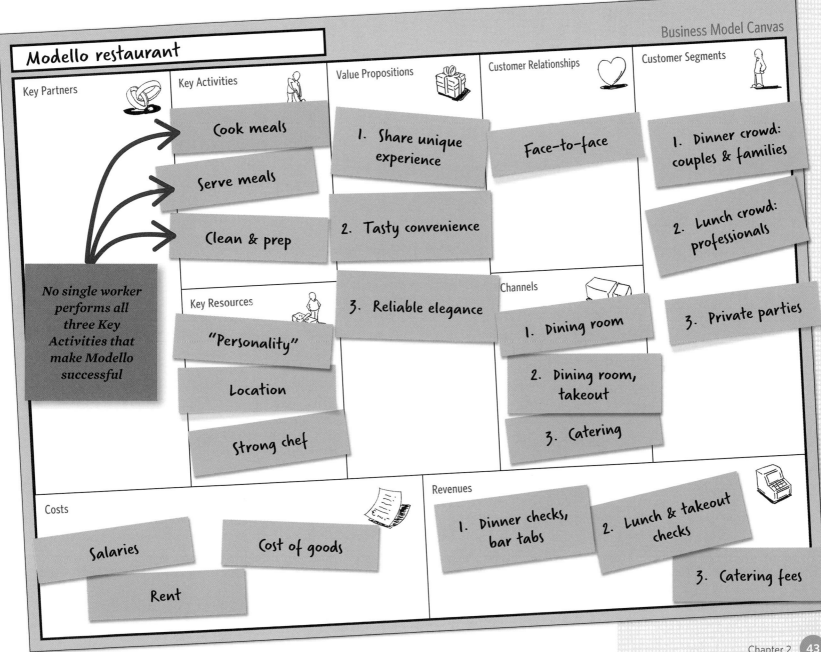

Modello restaurant

Business Model Canvas

Key Partners

Key Activities

Cook meals

Serve meals

Clean & prep

No single worker performs all three Key Activities that make Modello successful

Key Resources

"Personality"

Location

Strong chef

Value Propositions

1. Share unique experience

2. Tasty convenience

3. Reliable elegance

Customer Relationships

Face-to-face

Channels

1. Dining room

2. Dining room, takeout

3. Catering

Customer Segments

1. Dinner crowd: couples & families

2. Lunch crowd: professionals

3. Private parties

Costs

Salaries

Cost of goods

Rent

Revenues

1. Dinner checks, bar tabs

2. Lunch & takeout checks

3. Catering fees

Seeing the Whole

"Looking back, what we did was stupid," says soft-spoken entrepreneur Ben West. "We started a multinational organization to sell products to people who had no money!"

Yet four years after launching his unlikely venture, West's firm, EcoZoom, ranked #768 on the Inc. 5000 list of the fastest-growing private corporations in the United States.

West began his business career with a successful but unfulfilling stint as an account manager at a trucking corporation. Determined to improve his analytical and marketing skills, West left to pursue an MBA. He found himself drawn toward social ventures, and joined the university's entrepreneurship program, where he conceived the idea of producing a highly-efficient wood-burning stove for use in developing countries.

But West's model-and-test instincts clashed with the university's single-minded focus on business plan contests and fund-raising, and in an ironic twist, he was expelled from the entrepreneurship program.

Undeterred, West forged ahead with two partners and launched EcoZoom, a Certified B social venture. Since then, EcoZoom has delivered more than 650,000 stoves in 34 countries. The stoves are solid performers in their primary cooking function, but they also improve health, reduce noxious emissions, and save money for millions of people throughout the developing world.

"I need to see a business in its entirety, with every interdependency visible," West says. "The Canvas makes that possible. Equally important, it lets us account for non-financial benefits—the real purpose of our business."

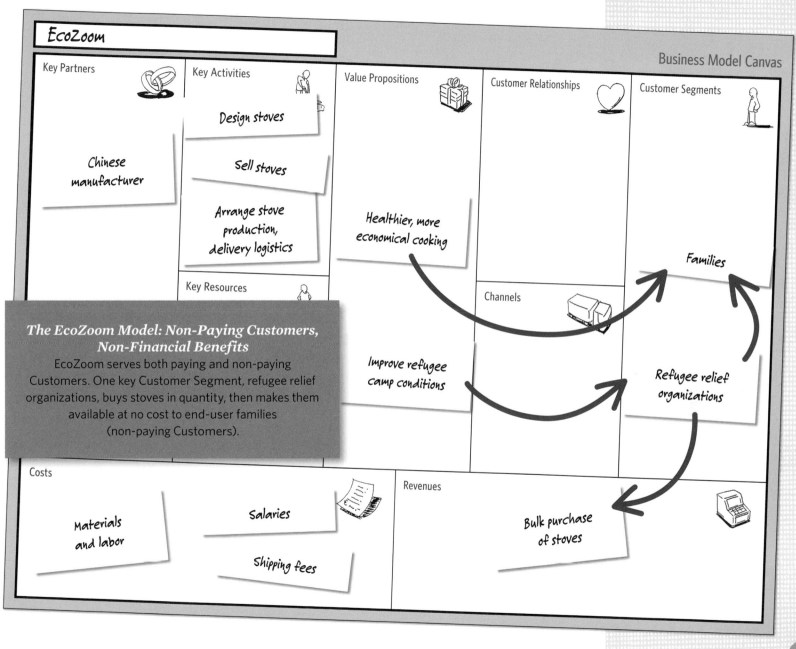

EcoZoom

Business Model Canvas

Key Partners

Chinese manufacturer

Key Activities

Design stoves

Sell stoves

Arrange stove production, delivery logistics

Key Resources

Value Propositions

Healthier, more economical cooking

Improve refugee camp conditions

Customer Relationships

Channels

Customer Segments

Families

Refugee relief organizations

The EcoZoom Model: Non-Paying Customers, Non-Financial Benefits
EcoZoom serves both paying and non-paying Customers. One key Customer Segment, refugee relief organizations, buys stoves in quantity, then makes them available at no cost to end-user families (non-paying Customers).

Costs

Materials and labor

Salaries

Shipping fees

Revenues

Bulk purchase of stoves

Externalities: Positive and Negative

As a social venture, non-financial benefits lie at the heart of EcoZoom's model and exemplify the company's purpose. For example, inhaling smoke from fires and unimproved stoves is like smoking two packs of cigarettes a day, and is linked to diseases that cause over four million deaths a year—more than malaria and tuberculosis combined. Moreover, smoke affects bystanders as well as users, so it is a *negative externality:* a cost affecting people who did not choose to incur that cost. EcoZoom stoves create a non-financial benefit (a *positive externality*) by dramatically reducing smoke.

Similarly, demand for wood fuel and charcoal contribute to deforestation, while smoke from inefficient cooking fires is filled with methane, CO_2 and other climate-altering gases. EcoZoom stoves reduce these emissions.

EcoZoom stoves generate positive externalities in several ways. For example, poor families can spend up to 30% of their monthly income to purchase propane or other conventional fuels, enforcing a cycle of energy poverty. Meanwhile, some women and girls spend hours each day gathering fuel, keeping them from more productive activities such as attending school. EcoZoom stoves lower conventional fuel costs and create more productive time for those who gather fuel.

You can easily account for positive externalities in a business model diagram by creating new building blocks below Revenue. Describe negative externalities under Costs.

Accounting for Externalities

Positive externalities and non-paying Customers may be key considerations if you work in government, healthcare, the military, or the legal, education, or nonprofit sectors. On the other hand, negative externalities, such as pollution and noise, may be important considerations if you work in industry. Use the Canvas to grasp the entirety of your business model.

Next, consider a different business that interacts with Customers entirely online—and most likely already counts you as a user!

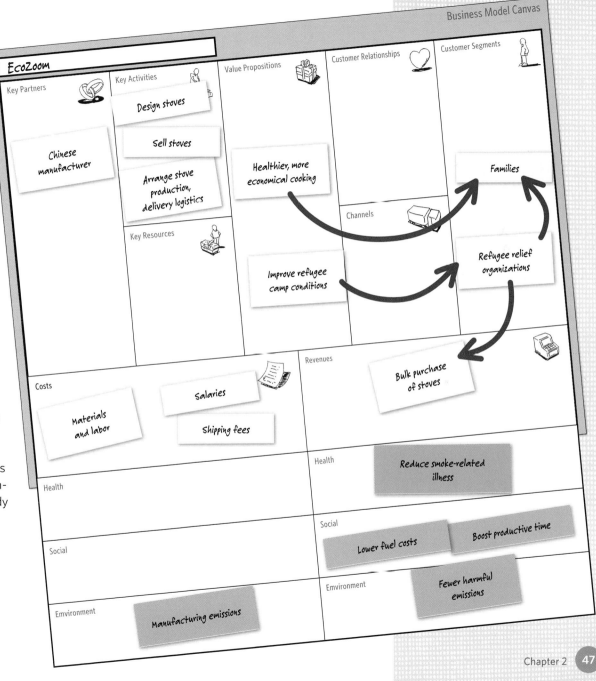

EcoZoom

Key Partners

Chinese manufacturer

Key Activities

Design stoves

Sell stoves

Arrange stove production, delivery logistics

Key Resources

Value Propositions

Healthier, more economical cooking

Improve refugee camp conditions

Customer Relationships

Channels

Customer Segments

Families

Refugee relief organizations

Costs

Materials and labor

Salaries

Shipping fees

Revenues

Bulk purchase of stoves

Health

Social

Emvironment

Manufacturing emissions

Health

Reduce smoke-related illness

Social

Lower fuel costs

Boost productive time

Emvironment

Fewer harmful emissions

An Online Model

Here is a business that may already serve you as a Customer: Facebook. Most people are familiar with Facebook, but how many understand how it works as an enterprise? Drawing Facebook's business model can be a real eye-opener.

Take a look at the Canvas on the facing page (to help you, hint questions appear inside each building block). Then, grab some sticky notes and a pen, and see if you can diagram Facebook's basic business model. Here are some hints:

- Think of Facebook's most basic service: ignore details for now
- Start by defining two distinct Customer Segments and their respective Value Propositions
- Use only one sticky note within each of the remaining building blocks. Each note should contain three words at most
- Ignore the Key Partners building block for now

After trying your hand at diagramming Facebook's business model, turn the page!

Facebook

Key Partners

- Who are our Key Partners?
- Which Key Resources do they supply, or which Key Activities do they perform?
- What do they offer that is indispensable to our model?
- Ways Key Partners create benefits:
  · Optimize or economize
  · Reduce risk or uncertainty
  · Provide otherwise unattainable resources or activities

Key Activities
- What Key Activities do our Value Propositions, Channels, Customer Relationships, and Revenue require?
- Types of Key Activities:
  Make: design, develop, manufacture, solve, deliver
  Sell: educate, advocate, demonstrate, promote, advertise
  Support: manage, maintain, supervise, otherwise assist people who make or sell

Key Resources
- What assets do our Value Propositions, Channels, Customer Relationships, and Revenue require?
- Four types of Key Resources:
  People: skilled workers
  Tangible Property: vehicles, buildings, land, equipment, tools
  Intangible Property: brands, methods, systems, software, patents, copyrights, licenses
  Money: cash, stock, receivables, lines of credit, financial guarantees

Costs

- What are our biggest Costs?
- Which Key Resources and Key Activities are most expensive?
- What negative externalities do we generate?
- Types of Costs:
  Fixed: salaries, leases
  Variable: cost of goods or services, contingent labor
  Non-cash: amortization, goodwill, externalities

Value Propositions

- What benefit(s) do we provide to Customers? For example:

Functional
- Reduced risk
- Lower cost
- Better convenience or usability
- Improved performance
- Getting a specific job done

Emotional
- Enjoyment or pleasure
- Acceptance
- Belonging
- Approval
- Security

Social
- Elevated status
- Taste, style validation
- Affinity

Customer Relationships

- How do we provide post-sales support? (Marketing Phase 5)
- What kinds of relationships do we have in place now?

  For example:
  - In-person or telephone assistance
  - Automated e-mail or self-service Web forms
  - Remote personal service via e-mail, chat, Skype, etc.
  - User community or wiki
  - Co creation with Customers
- What other relationships might Customers expect us to establish and maintain with them?

Channels

- Through which Channels do we reach Customers?
- Which Channels work best?
- Are there other Channels that Customers might prefer?
- Marketing Phases 1-4
  1. Awareness: How do prospects discover us?
  2. Evaluation: How do we induce evaluation?
  3. Purchase: How do Customers buy?
  4. Delivery: How do we deliver?

Customer Segments

- Whom do we benefit?
- Which Customers account for most of our Revenue?
- Strategically, who is our most important Customer?
- Who are our Customer's Customers?

Revenues

- For what benefits are our Customers truly willing to pay?
- How do they pay now?
- How might they prefer to pay?
- How much Revenue does each Customer contribute?
- What positive externalities do we generate?
- What forms do payments take?

  For example:
  - Asset sale
  - Lease or rental fee
  - Subscription charge

  - Licensing fee
  - Brokerage fee
  - Placement or advertising fee
  - Auction-based dynamic pricing

Facebook's Business Model

How did you do? Here are notes to help you think about one way Facebook's business model can be diagrammed:

Customer Segments

Facebook has two main Customer Segments: 1) consumers who pay nothing to use Facebook services, and 2) advertisers who pay fees to place advertisements, post sponsored content, or conduct market research. Facebook's business model depends on having hundreds of millions of non-paying users who collectively comprise a massive potential market for advertisers. Anyone who creates a Facebook account becomes a Customer. More than 99 percent of Customers pay nothing for services.

Value Proposition

The main benefit Facebook provides to consumers is the ability to "connect and share" with friends and family. The main benefit Facebook provides to advertisers is the opportunity to sell, expose their brands, perform targeted market research, or do other things ultimately aimed at attracting new Customers—or upselling current Customers.

Channels

Facebook communicates, sells, and delivers its Value Proposition exclusively through the Internet. Consumers use Facebook through a variety of devices (smartphones, tablets, personal computers). Note that Facebook, like most businesses, uses the same Channels to serve both new and existing Customers.

Customer Relationships

Facebook communicates with consumers (registered users) exclusively through automated text or e-mail messages. The company uses similarly automated messages and Web forms to communicate with smaller advertisers, and uses personalized e-mail, telephone, and in-person conversations to deal with bigger advertisers.

Revenues

Consumers pay nothing for Facebook services. Advertisers, on the other hand, pay placement fees to have their advertisements or other content shown to Facebook users. Most ads are bought directly by advertisers using self-service Web forms.

Key Resources

Facebook's platform (software, proprietary algorithms, databases, server arrays, and the Facebook.com branded Web site) is the company's single most important asset. Here is a thought experiment that can help identify Key Resources: What would happen tomorrow if Facebook fired 500 employees? Would the company collapse? Would its stock price crash? In contrast, what would happen tomorrow if Facebook's Web site suddenly became unavailable for two hours?

Key Activities

Protecting and developing the platform are Facebook's most important Key Activities. Remember, Key Activities are those activities essential to creating, selling, and delivering the Value Proposition. Activities such as accounting and maintaining internal computer systems, while important, are secondary.

Key Partners

Facebook does not appear to depend on partners to provide its core service (it has acquired a number of companies that previously might have served as Key Partners). For newer and more specialized services, application developers are Key Partners and/or Customers.

Costs

As with most enterprises, salaries are Facebook's biggest single cost. The company also incurs huge infrastructure and energy expenses.

Now, get ready to use the Business Model Canvas in *your* organization.

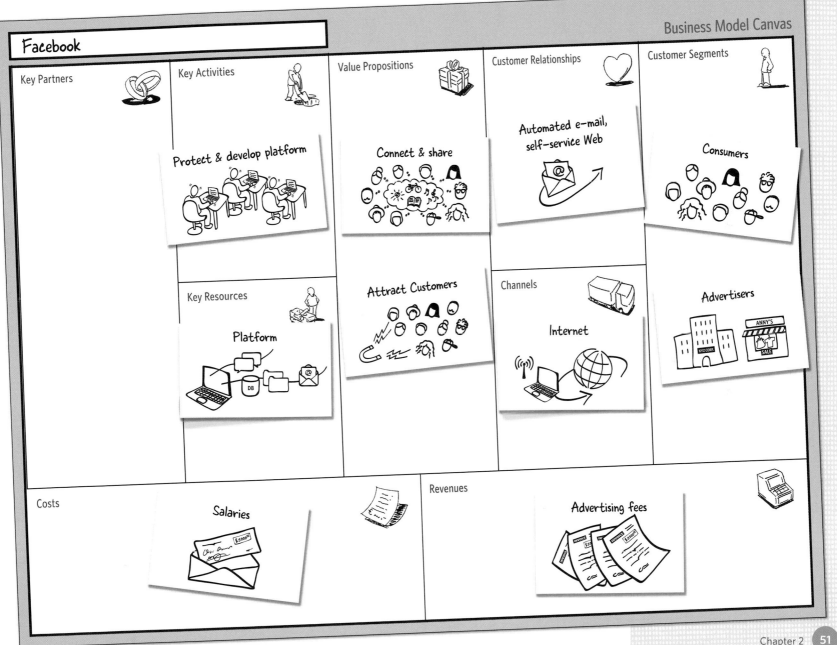

Business Model Canvas

Facebook

Key Partners

Key Activities

Protect & develop platform

Key Resources

Platform

Value Propositions

Connect & share

Attract Customers

Customer Relationships

Automated e-mail, self-service Web

Channels

Internet

Customer Segments

Consumers

Advertisers

Costs

Salaries

Revenues

Advertising fees

How to Work with the Canvas

Did you notice how seeing Facebook in business model terms provided a view of the company that contrasts with popular perception? Grasping the centrality of Facebook's platform, and its highly automated Channel and Customer Relationships, gives a far more realistic, grounded understanding of how the company actually works. Unless Facebook's business model is examined in a logical, rigorous way, our understanding is likely to remain based on assumptions rather than facts.

That said, diagramming a business model usually means recording both facts and assumptions. Getting a model "right" is less important than teaching and using a common vocabulary to define an organization's overarching logic. That logic may well include assumptions that must be verified later.

Here are some general guidelines on using the Business Model Canvas:

Work BIG
Print Canvases at A1 size (about 24" x 36") or larger. Working big expands thinking and makes collaborating with others easier. Avoid standard-size papers (A4/letter) that people work with daily.

Collaborate
When drawing and analyzing a business model, team up with colleagues and/or Customers, suppliers, prospects, or third-party experts. Gathering people who represent different perspectives (different ages, occupations, functional areas within the enterprise, etc.) produces better results. *Use your Canvas sessions to model the kind of collaborative behavior you want to encourage in your workplace.*

Write on Sticky Notes
Write on sticky notes, not on the Canvas itself. Sticky notes let you easily change, discard, or move items to different places—and they remind everyone that business models change (and expire!).

Use Drawings

Use simple drawings when you can. Label them with words for additional clarity.

ENTREPRENEURS

Write One Idea per Note

Write one clear, concise idea per note. Do not use multiple bullet points on a single note: keep ideas separate and thereby movable.

Use Color to Create Meaningful Patterns, Not to Decorate

Use different-colored sticky notes to make meaningful distinctions between different Customer Segments, between facts and assumptions, or to suggest a modification to a particular building block, etc. Avoid using color merely for decoration.

Avoid "Orphan" Notes

All sticky notes should be related to elements in other building blocks—none should be "orphaned."

Use Precise Language

Use precise language. For example,Key Activities should be verbs: use **sell** rather than **sales**.

Keep Canvases Simple when Starting Out

Keep Canvases simple and uncluttered when diagramming a business model for the first time. Once you have captured the logic at a high level, you can add detail.

Use Thick-Tip Black Markers, not Pens or Pencils

Use thick-tip black markers rather than pens or pencils to write on sticky notes. This makes reading easier when collaborators are standing away from the Canvas.

Work on Walls Rather than Tables

Work on walls rather than tables whenever possible. People think better on their feet!

Distinguish Between Facts and Hypotheses

Distinguish between facts and hypotheses (assumptions). Doing so reminds everyone that hypotheses must eventually be tested.

Stay in the Same Tense

Avoid mixing present, past, and future scenarios in the same Canvas. Stay in the same tense: make separate Canvases for past, present, and future scenarios.

Present Canvases One Note at a Time

When presenting a Canvas to other team members, start with a blank Canvas and add notes one at a time as you tell a business model "story," building block by building block. This is far more effective than sequentially pointing at multiple notes already stuck to the Canvas.

Things to Try on Monday Morning

Try Modeling Your Enterprise

Now it is your turn: use the Business Model Canvas on these two pages to diagram the business model of the enterprise for which you work. To help you, hint questions appear inside each building block. Alternatively, you can print out the Canvas poster (available for free when you sign up at BusinessModelsForTeams.com). The poster includes hint questions (in tiny type that encourages you to print and work BIG!).

Key Partners

- Who are our Key Partners?
- Which Key Resources do they supply, or which Key Activities do they perform?
- What do they offer that is indispensable to our model?
- Ways Key Partners create benefits:
- Optimize or economize
- Reduce risk or uncertainty
- Provide otherwise unattainable resources or activities

Key Activities

- What Key Activities do our Value Propositions, Channels, Customer Relationships, and Revenue require?
- Types of Key Activities:
  Make: design, develop, manufacture, solve, deliver
  Sell: educate, advocate, demonstrate, promote, advertise
  Support: manage, maintain, supervise, otherwise assist people who make or sell

Key Resources

- What assets do our Value Propositions, Channels, Customer Relationships, and Revenue require?
- Four types of Key Resources:
  People: skilled workers
  Tangible Property: vehicles, buildings, land, equipment, tools
  Intangible Property: brands, methods, systems, software, patents, copyrights, licenses
  Money: cash, stock, receivables, lines of credit, financial guarantees

Costs

- What are our biggest Costs?
- Which Key Resources and Key Activities are most expensive?
- What negative externalities do we generate?
- Types of Costs:
  Fixed: salaries, leases
  Variable: cost of goods or services, contingent labor
  Non-cash: amortization, goodwill, externalities

Value Propositions

- What benefit(s) do we provide to Customers? For example:

Functional
- · Reduced risk
- · Lower cost
- · Better convenience or usability
- · Improved performance
- · Getting a specific job done

Emotional
- · Enjoyment or pleasure
- · Acceptance
- · Belonging
- · Approval
- · Security

Social
- · Elevated status
- · Taste, style validation
- · Affinity

Customer Relationships

- How do we provide post-sales support? (Marketing Phase 5)
- What kinds of relationships do we have in place now?

  For example:
  - • In-person or telephone assistance
  - • Automated e-mail or self-service Web forms
  - • Remote personal service via e-mail, chat, Skype, etc.
  - • User community or wiki
  - • Co-creation with Customers
- What other relationships might Customers expect us to establish and maintain with them?

Channels

- Through which Channels do we reach Customers?
- Which Channels work best?
- Are there other Channels that Customers might prefer?
- Marketing Phases 1-4
  1. Awareness: How do prospects discover us?
  2. Evaluation: How do we induce evaluation?
  3. Purchase: How do Customers buy?
  4. Delivery: How do we deliver?

Customer Segments

- Whom do we benefit?
- Which Customers account for most of our Revenue?
- Strategically, who is our most important Customer?
- Who are our Customer's Customers?

Revenues

- For what benefits are our Customers truly willing to pay?
- How do they pay now?
- How might they prefer to pay?
- How much Revenue does each Customer contribute?
- What positive externalities do we generate?
- What forms do payments take?

  For example:
  - · Asset sale
  - · Lease or rental fee
  - · Subscription charge
  - · Licensing fee
  - · Brokerage fee
  - · Placement or advertising fee
  - · Auction-based dynamic pricing

Next Steps for You and Your Team

Wouldn't any organization want all its workers to understand its business model? Wouldn't any organization want its business model to appear in its employee handbook, and be enthusiastically taught at every new employee orientation?

Well, few organizations take business modeling that far. Most still seem to believe that business modeling is important only for strategists and executives. But you are about to meet a number of forward-thinking organizations that use business modeling to bolster teamwork, attract and engage talented workers, boost retention, and improve both employee and Customer satisfaction.

Business modeling enthusiasts who work for larger organizations may feel frustrated by top management's failure to articulate the enterprise business model and proactively teach it throughout the organization. Is this the case where you work?

You may not be positioned to ensure organization-wide teaching of the enterprise model. But you may be in a position to define your own team's business model and ensure that every member understands it—and more important, uses that team model to guide everyday action.

The next chapters show exactly how to do that.

Chapter 3

Modeling Teams

Whom Do I Help?

Every enterprise has a business model, and the Business Model Canvas shows at a glance how that enterprise works. Similarly, most enterprises consist of teams, and the Business Model Canvas can show at a glance how each team within the enterprise works. This chapter explains how to diagram team business models. Start by answering two crucial questions all workers must ask themselves. The first question is, *Whom do I help*? In other words, *Who is my Customer?*

Who is my Customer?

Think of your own work situation. Your main Customer is *whoever makes the decision to purchase your services*. If you are an employee of the Modello restaurant, for example, Steve Brown is your main Customer, because he decided to purchase your services by hiring you. Steve is an internal Customer, because you and he work for the same organization.

Now, who are Steve's main Customers? Steve's main Customers are Modello *diners*, because they decide to purchase meals at his restaurant. Diners are external Customers, because they do not work for the same organization as Steve.

Whom do I help? is a crucial question, *because few people gain true satisfaction by helping only themselves*. Deep down, people yearn to help others through their work. Helping others activates one of the four key human motivators: Purpose.

Purpose is easiest to spot with external Customers. At Modello, for example, waiters and hostesses experience firsthand helping diners enjoy a special night out, or facilitating group bonding at a gracefully catered dinner. But people who serve internal Customers, like cooks and dishwashers, can have a harder time seeing how their work helps others.

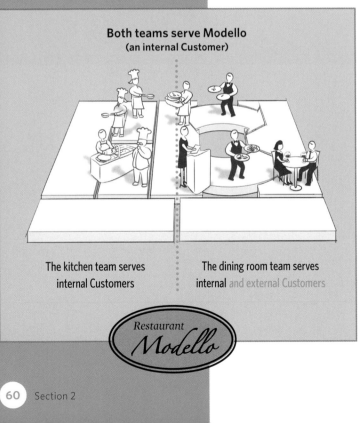

Both teams serve Modello
(an internal Customer)

The kitchen team serves internal Customers

The dining room team serves internal and external Customers

Restaurant **Modello**

How Do I Help?

A dishwasher, for example, understands that he helps the restaurant. But to him, the restaurant may be an impersonal entity. When the dishwasher understands *whom* he helps—the cooks and servers he sees every day at work—the *whom* becomes personal. That is why it is so important that each worker understands how their work benefits specific team members, not just the enterprise.

The second crucial question all workers must ask themselves is, *How do I help?* When a dishwasher understands how cooks and servers depend on clean cookware and dishes to do their own jobs, he understands teamwork's core: *interdependency*. By helping his teammates, he gains a greater sense of purpose and job satisfaction. Over time, he begins to see how his activities contribute to the success of the restaurant.

The teamwork table here describes each kitchen team member's role, tasks, Customers served, results of task success, and consequences of task failure.

Kitchen Team Teamwork Table

Role	Tasks	Internal Customers	Result of task success	Consequence of task failure
Chef	Design, update excellent menu	Modello (Steve)	Good reputation, financial success	Reputational/financial loss
	Train and supervise	Cooks	Better professional skills, bigger tips*	Smaller tips, poor social media reviews*
	Explain menu, train servers to recommend dishes, prevent allergic reactions	Servers	Repeat external Customers, bigger tips*	Lost external Customers, smaller tips, poor social media reviews*
Cooks	Correctly and consistently prepare menu items	Modello (Steve)	Good reputation, financial success	Reputational/financial loss
	Correctly and consistently prepare menu items	Servers	Repeat external Customers, bigger tips*	Lost external Customers, smaller tips, poor social media reviews*
Dishwasher	Promptly and thoroughly wash dinnerware, cookware	Modello (Steve)	Positive image	Poor image
	Promptly and thoroughly wash cookware	Cooks	Work proceeds smoothly	Delayed work, frustration
	Promptly and thoroughly wash dinnerware	Servers	Eliminate cleanliness-related complaints, bigger tips*	Unpredictable dining experience, loss of Customers, smaller tips, unfavorable social media postings*

*Ripple-through effect from external Customers

One of a leader's most important tasks is to help others see why their work matters to someone.[1] People who grasp teamwork—who they help and how they help—have built a foundation for self-organization and self-direction. Next, learn how to use the Canvas to draw a team business model.

How to Diagram a Team Business Model

Diagramming a team business model is straightforward. But that is not the same as easy!

Start by defining your team's Customers. This is the most important step in creating your team business model, because most of us do not think of our colleagues as Customers. But if someone else relies on your team's output, they are a Customer.

The kitchen team model on the opposite page shows three Customers: 1) Modello (Steve), 2) the dining room team, and 3) diners. Everyone on the kitchen team agreed to create revenue for Modello when they were hired. Diners are also Customers, of course, even though they are served indirectly. This Canvas suggests that diners are actually direct Customers of the dining room staff, a relationship indicated by the curved arrow pointing from the dining room team to diners. In this sense, the kitchen team's most important Customer is the dining room staff, who directly serve external Customers.

Diners could be considered the most important Customers for *everyone* who works for Modello, because most revenue—and therefore wages—comes from diners. Business model thinking suggests, though, that the best way to serve external Customers is *by first serving the enterprise and internal teams that col-lectively deliver value to those Customers*. Remember this book's goal is *to improve teamwork and help people avoid poor decisions*. Use the tools flexibly, in accordance with the philosophy of your organization.

After defining your Customers, list a separate Value Proposition for each. Numbering the sticky notes can be helpful. Once you have defined Customers and Value Propositions, filling out the rest of the model is usually straightforward. Note that this Canvas shows Steve in two roles: as Customer and as Key Partner. The Canvas also shows the dining room team in two roles. When drawing a business model, a person or group can serve in more than one role.

List financial costs in your team business model if you receive a budget allocation from the organization (or a higher-level team) and can make hires, purchases, engage consultants, and so forth. Otherwise, as in this simple kitchen team example, Costs reflect non-financial elements.

After reviewing the kitchen team model on the opposite page, consider four team model examples from the finance, software, energy, and consulting sectors on the following pages.

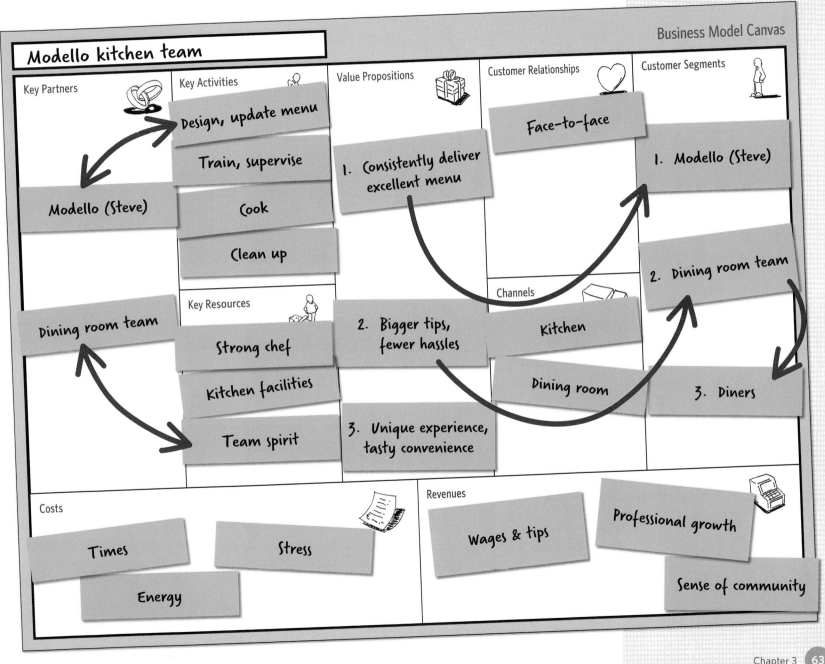

Business Model Canvas

Modello kitchen team

Key Partners

Modello (Steve)

Dining room team

Key Activities

Design, update menu

Train, supervise

Cook

Clean up

Key Resources

Strong chef

Kitchen facilities

Team spirit

Value Propositions

1. Consistently deliver excellent menu

2. Bigger tips, fewer hassles

3. Unique experience, tasty convenience

Customer Relationships

Face-to-face

Channels

Kitchen

Dining room

Customer Segments

1. Modello (Steve)

2. Dining room team

3. Diners

Costs

Times

Stress

Energy

Revenues

Wages & tips

Professional growth

Sense of community

The DBA Team

A Paradigm Shift for Finance Professionals

DBA Group is a ten-person consultancy that provides interim and part-time financial director services, including fundraising, to early-stage technology companies in Cambridge, UK. In other words, they can serve as chief financial officers for organizations too new to hire one. Over the past 20 years DBA has helped more than 50 companies raise more than U.S. $500 million.

Over the years, founder David Blair struggled with a recurring problem: entrepreneurs and investors often see finance people as backward-looking paperwork experts: compiling data, doing tax and compliance work, and needing to be advised of decisions only after the fact. David wanted entrepreneurs and investors to see his small, on-site teams of experts as key contributors to the decision-making process. That way, they could generate more value for clients.

David knew he needed to address the problem with his own teams. "Being 'process people,' finance professionals tend to focus on their activities and outputs rather than the value they provide, especially because they usually work with internal rather than external clients. The team Canvas really helped them achieve that paradigm shift," he says.

Put simply, a DBA team's Value Proposition is to help a client's investors and senior management team "sleep well at night," says David. That means accurately tracking the progress of both financial and non-financial key performance indicators (KPIs), checking these against plans, and accurately predicting the impact of change—both positive and negative—in the business environment. That is more valuable than mere assurances about compliance and tax returns.

The Key Activities required for team members to create true value include getting out of their comfort zones for more face-to face meetings and working with the client to identify nonfinancial goals to track. The team then must build systems to capture and report KPI data in a concise and usable format. That requires good IT resources and appropriate training. More important, though, team members need to adopt the correct attitude, says David. They must truly engage clients, grasp pain points, and communicate and deliver solid value. For their part, clients are both Customers and Key Partners: after buying into the interim financial team concept, they must advocate it internally and invite DBA staff to the right meetings.

"Having used personal business models for individuals on the teams, it was an easy extension to use team models," says David.

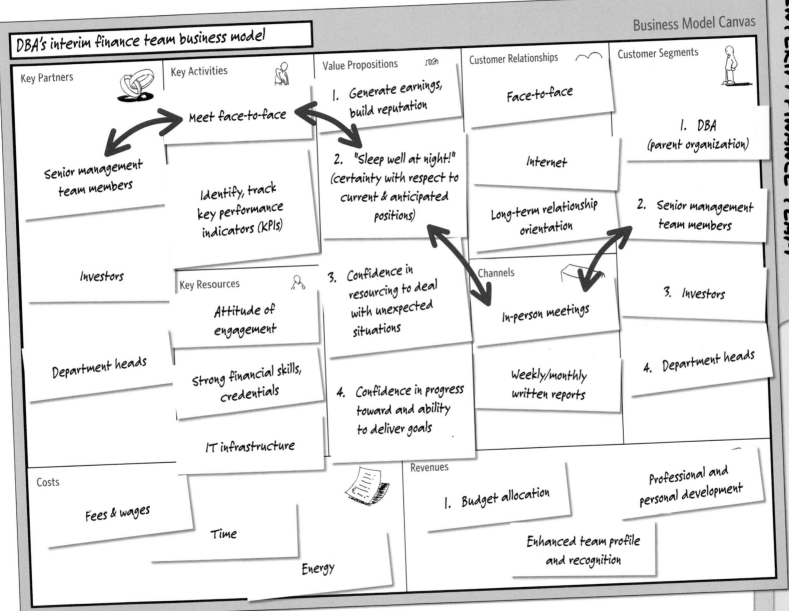

DBA's interim finance team business model

Business Model Canvas

Key Partners

Senior management team members

Investors

Department heads

Key Activities

Meet face-to-face

Identify, track key performance indicators (KPIs)

Key Resources

Attitude of engagement

Strong financial skills, credentials

IT infrastructure

Value Propositions

1. Generate earnings, build reputation

2. "Sleep well at night!" (certainty with respect to current & anticipated positions)

3. Confidence in resourcing to deal with unexpected situations

4. Confidence in progress toward and ability to deliver goals

Customer Relationships

Face-to-face

Internet

Long-term relationship orientation

Channels

In-person meetings

Weekly/monthly written reports

Customer Segments

1. DBA (parent organization)

2. Senior management team members

3. Investors

4. Department heads

Costs

Fees & wages

Time

Energy

Revenues

1. Budget allocation

Enhanced team profile and recognition

Professional and personal development

Viewpoint Software:
Learning Services Team Model

Beth Allen

Viewpoint Construction Software provides construction management, estimating, and Enterprise Resource Planning (ERP) software to the global construction and contractor industry. Headquartered in Portland, Oregon, Viewpoint employs approximately 700 people in the U.S., UK, and Australia.

Beth Allen serves as Viewpoint's Director of Learning Services, the team responsible for teaching Viewpoint clients how to use its products and services. Beth's team creates and maintains self-service content (help pages, videos, quick reference guides, and so forth), all of which is available to Customers online at no charge. The team also offers fee-based Customer training and manages five certification programs for internal and external software consultants who service and support Viewpoint products.

When Viewpoint's long-time CEO retired and other key executives left, Beth found herself facing an entirely new executive leadership team that was not fully aware of Learning Services' role. To demonstrate Learning Services' value, Beth decided to create a team business model. Diagramming the team model and describing it aloud to a colleague illuminated an important conflict.

"Our mission is to reduce the load on the live customer support team through effective training and self-service access to expertise," says Beth. "But when learners encounter outdated online content in the Customer portal, they place more calls to the live support center, increasing costs. Outdated content 'costs' my team nothing—but it is expensive for Customer Support! The team model shows these interdependencies and makes a strong business case for investing in updating or purging outdated learning management system content."

Beth discovered another practical benefit of using a team business model. "I stopped writing lists of important items and switched to describing things in the context of a business model. People now see when something is a real priority. To-do task lists provide no context. The team business model is something I can use to educate others, especially our new executive team."

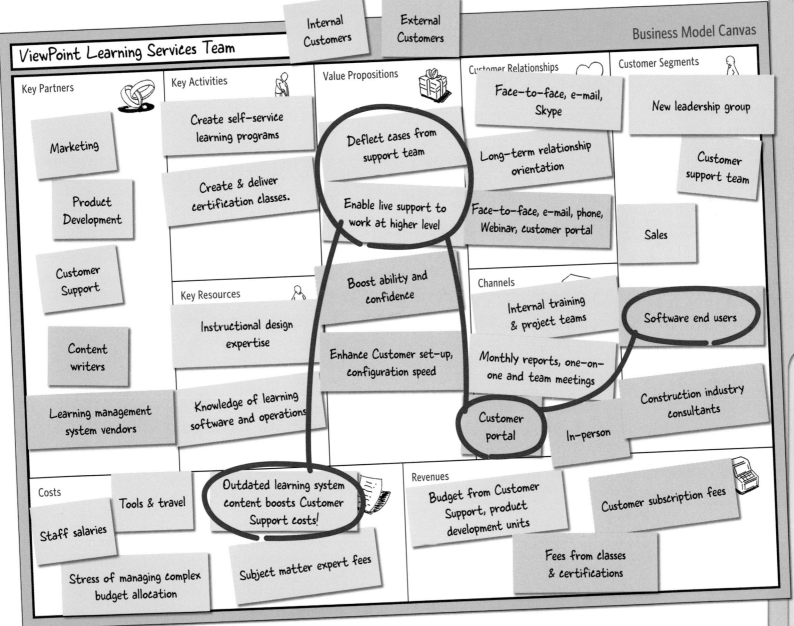

ViewPoint Learning Services Team

Business Model Canvas

Internal Customers

External Customers

Key Partners

Marketing

Product Development

Customer Support

Content writers

Learning management system vendors

Key Activities

Create self-service learning programs

Create & deliver certification classes.

Key Resources

Instructional design expertise

Knowledge of learning software and operations

Value Propositions

Deflect cases from support team

Enable live support to work at higher level

Boost ability and confidence

Enhance Customer set-up, configuration speed

Customer Relationships

Face-to-face, e-mail, Skype

Long-term relationship orientation

Face-to-face, e-mail, phone, Webinar, customer portal

Channels

Internal training & project teams

Monthly reports, one-on-one and team meetings

Customer portal

In-person

Customer Segments

New leadership group

Customer support team

Sales

Software end users

Construction industry consultants

Costs

Tools & travel

Staff salaries

Stress of managing complex budget allocation

Subject matter expert fees

Outdated learning system content boosts Customer Support costs!

Revenues

Budget from Customer Support, product development units

Fees from classes & certifications

Customer subscription fees

67

Team Model Supports Enterprise Model Shift

Isabella Panizza

Enel of Italy is an electrical energy producer that serves more than 60 million households in over 30 countries and boasts the largest customer base of any energy producer in Europe. In 2015, Fortune ranked Enel fifth among its top 50 "change the world" companies, ahead of Facebook, Alibaba, and IBM.

That same year Enel began planning a new strategic platform for growth called Open Power. Open Power was designed to pioneer a "participatory" industry model whereby users can produce energy and engage Enel via its fully digitized grid and an open Internet platform. Isabella Panizza was assigned the challenging task of developing the digital implementation of the company's new brand positioning, which had been launched to support Enel's Open Power operational strategy.

Isabella turned to Beople, a company specializing in business model innovation, for help. Beople used both team and personal business models.

The project started with a series of trainings delivered to Enel business-unit and digital team leaders around the world. Participants drew their own personal business models, including jobs-to-be-done and pains and gains.[2] This clarified the new team's key Customer segments and related Value Propositions, and enabled the design of the team business model shown on the facing page.

Next, roles and processes were defined to facilitate hiring people for the new Open Power digital implementation team. Once new team members were on board, Isabella co-facilitated a workshop where participants used the Alignment Canvas (see page 78) to define their team roles. Then, participants used the Branding Canvas, a tool created by Beople's founder, to define how they would spread the Open Power message throughout Enel. Open Power launched successfully in 2016 and is now the face of the company.

Isabella says she derived the most satisfaction from seeing internal stakeholders understand her new team's role as a Key Partner. "Working with this methodology, the visual tools, and the common language they enable has been a powerful accelerator of the whole process," she says.

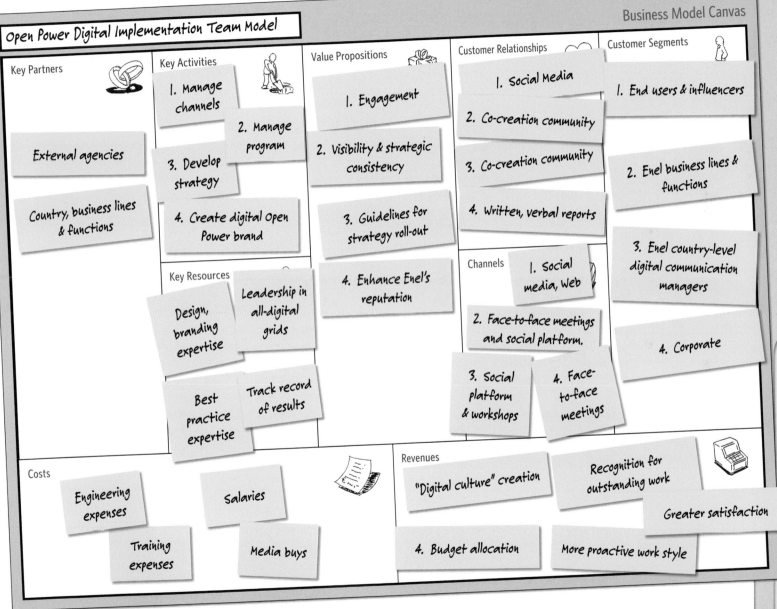

Open Power Digital Implementation Team Model

Key Partners

External agencies

Country, business lines & functions

Key Activities

1. Manage channels
2. Manage program
3. Develop strategy
4. Create digital Open Power brand

Key Resources

Design, branding expertise

Leadership in all-digital grids

Best practice expertise

Track record of results

Value Propositions

1. Engagement
2. Visibility & strategic consistency
3. Guidelines for strategy roll-out
4. Enhance Enel's reputation

Customer Relationships

1. Social Media
2. Co-creation community
3. Co-creation community
4. Written, verbal reports

Channels

1. Social media, Web
2. Face-to-face meetings and social platform.
3. Social platform & workshops
4. Face-to-face meetings

Customer Segments

1. End users & influencers
2. Enel business lines & functions
3. Enel country-level digital communication managers
4. Corporate

Costs

Engineering expenses

Salaries

Training expenses

Media buys

Revenues

"Digital culture" creation

Recognition for outstanding work

Greater satisfaction

4. Budget allocation

More proactive work style

69

An Internal Consulting Team at EY

Reinhard Dalz

An organization that employs more than 200,000 people faces staggering complexity—and provides a fertile internal learning laboratory for Reinhard Dalz, who works at EY (formerly Ernst & Young).

Reinhard is a senior manager for EY's People Advisory Services, a group that consults with clients on human resource issues. But People Advisory Services is also responsible for internally developing and testing new ways to build better workplaces. With encouragement from colleague Markus Heinen, EY's Chief Innovation Officer for Germany, Switzerland, and Austria, Reinhard started experimenting internally with team and personal business models.

"We have long used business models for external strategy, because client business models are often disrupted by economic, social, or technology trends," says Reinhard. "But we discovered that using team business models internally is a powerful way to help EY departments."

Reinhard created an internal consulting team (facing page) devoted to supporting the Chief Operating Offi-

cers (COO) who run departments that serve external EY clients. Reinhard and his colleagues found that compared to organization charts, the new group's team business model is far more effective for conveying understanding and purpose.

"We implicitly understood the new team's critical success factors, but had never clearly expressed them until we created a team business model. The team model is a far more powerful descriptive tool than an organization chart—explaining things and assuring alignment is far easier," says Reinhard. "Plus, the team business model helps new members identify the skills they need and the real value to be delivered."

Reinhard and his colleagues are now experimenting with personal business models that describe individual roles within the internal consulting team. "A personal business model clarifies expectations and skill profiles," he says, "and ensures that a person's individual goals match group aims."

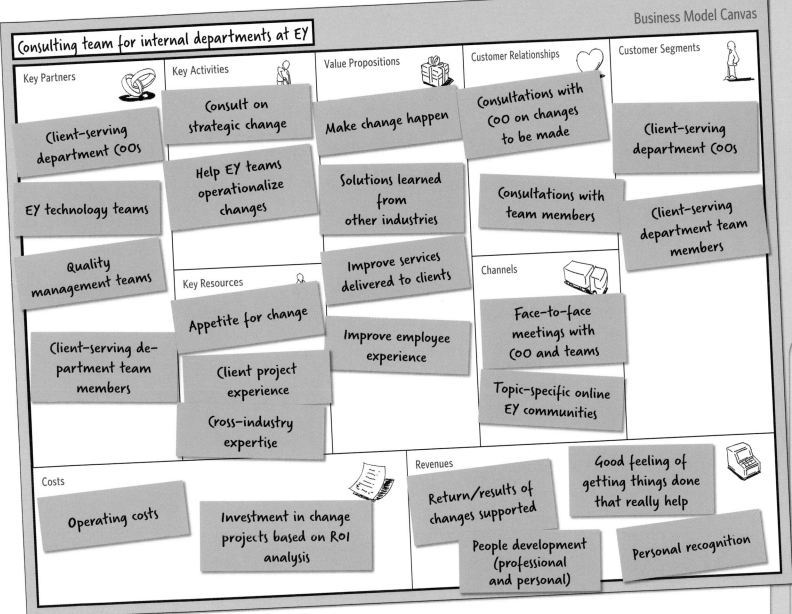

Consulting team for internal departments at EY

Key Partners

Client-serving department COOs

EY technology teams

Quality management teams

Client-serving department team members

Key Activities

Consult on strategic change

Help EY teams operationalize changes

Key Resources

Appetite for change

Client project experience

Cross-industry expertise

Value Propositions

Make change happen

Solutions learned from other industries

Improve services delivered to clients

Improve employee experience

Customer Relationships

Consultations with COO on changes to be made

Consultations with team members

Channels

Face-to-face meetings with COO and teams

Topic-specific online EY communities

Customer Segments

Client-serving department COOs

Client-serving department team members

Costs

Operating costs

Investment in change projects based on ROI analysis

Revenues

Return/results of changes supported

People development (professional and personal)

Good feeling of getting things done that really help

Personal recognition

Draw Your Team's Business Model

Now it is your turn. Grab some sticky notes and use the blank Canvas on the opposite page to draw your team's business model. Better yet, print out a poster-sized Canvas and draw the model together with your team. Here are some reminders to help you along:

1. Customers
If you have more than one Customer, numbering the sticky notes will help you indicate priority and match Customers to Value Propositions. Or, you could use different colored sticky notes for different Customers.

2. Value Proposition(s)
Each Customer should have a separate Value Proposition. Be sure to state your Value Proposition in terms of a benefit, solution, or outcome rather than in terms of an activity.

3. Channels and Customer Relationships
Different Customers may require different Channels or Customer Relationships. Use numbers or different colored notes.

4. Key Activities
Name specific activities required to create and deliver the Value Proposition (hint: these are often activities people want to avoid!). Leave out administrative or routine tasks.

5. Key Resources
What do you need to create and deliver your Value Proposition? Pay attention to essential elements that are missing or underdeveloped.

6. Key Partners
Include both internal and external partners. Specify what they will provide or what they will do. As in David Blair's case on page 64, note the critical role Key Partners can play in forging relationships.

7. Revenues and Costs
Note professional development and other non-financial benefits that team members will enjoy.

Once you have created a team model, it is time to discover how it relates to other teams. Learn how Beatriz used team models to reposition her own group—and discover an entirely new set of internal Customers.

Key Partners

- Who are our Key Partners?
- Which Key Resources do they supply, or which Key Activities do they perform?
- What do they offer that is indispensable to our model?
- Ways Key Partners create benefits:
  · Optimize or economize
  · Reduce risk or uncertainty
  · Provide otherwise unattainable resources or activities

Key Activities

- What Key Activities do our Value Propositions, Channels, Customer Relationships, and Revenue require?
- Types of Key Activities:
  Make: design, develop, manufacture, solve, deliver
  Sell: educate, advocate, demonstrate, promote, advertise
  Support: manage, maintain, supervise, otherwise assist people who make or sell

Key Resources

- What assets do our Value Propositions, Channels, Customer Relationships, and Revenue require?
- Four types of Key Resources:
  People: skilled workers
  Tangible Property: vehicles, buildings, land, equipment, tools
  Intangible Property: brands, methods, systems, software, patents, copyrights, licenses
  Money: cash, stock, receivables, lines of credit, financial guarantees

Value Propositions

- What benefit(s) do we provide to Customers? For example:
  Functional
  · Reduced risk
  · Lower cost
  · Better convenience or usability
  · Improved performance
  · Getting a specific job done
  Emotional
  · Enjoyment or pleasure
  · Acceptance
  · Belonging
  · Approval
  · Security
  Social
  · Elevated status
  · Taste, style validation
  · Affinity

Customer Relationships

- How do we provide post-sales support? (Marketing Phase 5)
- What kinds of relationships do we have in place now?
  For example:
  · In-person or telephone assistance
  · Automated e-mail or self-service Web forms
  · Remote personal service via e-mail, chat, Skype, etc.
  · User community or wiki
  · Co-creation with Customers
- What other relationships might Customers expect us to establish and maintain with them?

Channels

- Through which Channels do we reach Customers?
- Which Channels work best?
- Are there other Channels that Customers might prefer?
- Marketing Phases 1-4
  1. Awareness: How do prospects discover us?
  2. Evaluation: How do we induce evaluation?
  3. Purchase: How do Customers buy?
  4. Delivery: How do we deliver?

Customer Segments

- Whom do we benefit?
- Which Customers account for most of our Revenue?
- Strategically, who is our most important Customer?
- Who are our Customer's Customers?

Costs

- What are our biggest Costs?
- Which Key Resources and Key Activities are most expensive?
- What negative externalities do we generate?
- Types of Costs:
  Fixed: salaries, leases
  Variable: cost of goods or services, contingent labor
  Non-cash: amortization, goodwill, externalities

Revenues

- For what benefits are our Customers truly willing to pay?
- How do they pay now?
- How might they prefer to pay?
- How much Revenue does each Customer contribute?
- What positive externalities do we generate?
- What forms do payments take?
  For example:
  · Asset sale
  · Lease or rental fee
  · Subscription charge
  · Licensing fee
  · Brokerage fee
  · Placement or advertising fee
  · Auction-based dynamic pricing

Beatriz A. González Torre

Aligning a Team With Customer Goals

Beatriz Torre leads a training team that serves the 800-employee Elevator Innovation Center, a research and development division within Thyssen Krupp, a diversified global industrial giant with more than 150,000 employees and U.S. $42 billion in sales. The training team's purpose is simple: develop Innovation Center employee skills so they can deliver the increasingly complex ThyssenKrupp moving walkway and elevator systems used in buildings, airports, and large commercial centers around the world.

In her work as leader of the training team, Beatriz faced two related challenges.

First, amid growing budget scrutiny, she needed to demonstrate to the Elevator Innovation Center—an internal Customer—how her training team boosted research and development success. Second, she wanted to discover new ways her team could contribute and create additional value. Said Beatriz, "We needed to view things differently so that we could show who benefits from our work."

Beatriz decided to try aligning her team's business model with the Innovation Center's business model. First, she gave the Innovation Center programs manager an overview of business model thinking. Then, together they worked on a team Canvas for the Innovation Center. Next, she defined her training team's model. Finally, she placed the Innovation Center's team model atop her training team model to compare the two.

Read on to see how a significant mismatch—and a big opportunity—immediately became clear.

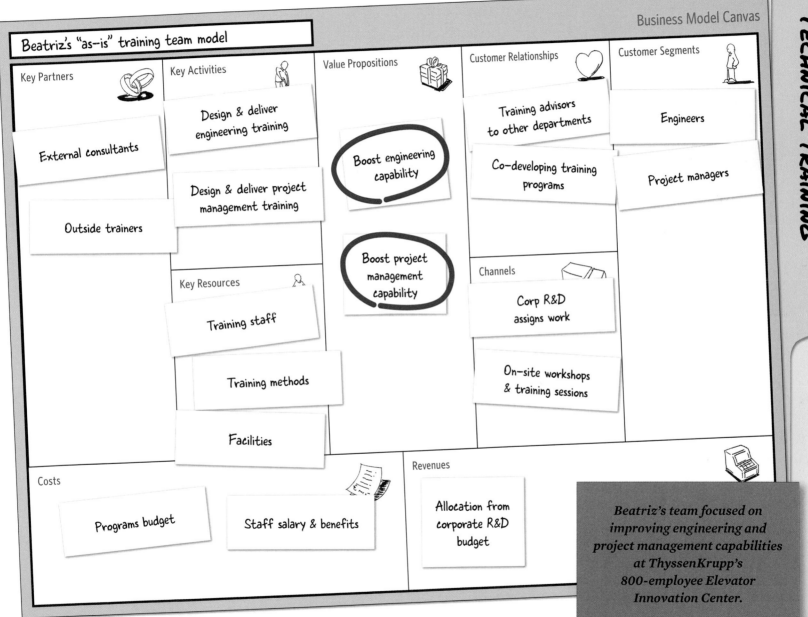

Beatriz's "as-is" training team model

Key Partners

External consultants

Outside trainers

Key Activities

Design & deliver engineering training

Design & deliver project management training

Key Resources

Training staff

Training methods

Facilities

Value Propositions

Boost engineering capability

Boost project management capability

Customer Relationships

Training advisors to other departments

Co-developing training programs

Channels

Corp R&D assigns work

On-site workshops & training sessions

Customer Segments

Engineers

Project managers

Costs

Programs budget

Staff salary & benefits

Revenues

Allocation from corporate R&D budget

Beatriz's team focused on improving engineering and project management capabilities at ThyssenKrupp's 800-employee Elevator Innovation Center.

Seeing Interconnections Unlocks Value

The Innovation Center's Value Proposition was "bring new products to market." But Beatriz and the manager's visualization of the Center's model clearly showed that creating new products demanded tight coordination with four other ThyssenKrupp teams: manufacturing, supply chain, sales, and finance. Yet members of these five interconnected teams had little *product* management expertise—and Beatriz's team had focused exclusively on engineering and project management training!

Beatriz immediately saw a strong need for *product* management training—and the need to provide that training to four other ThyssenKrupp teams, not just to the Innovation Center. This meant adding four new Customers, creating a new Value Proposition, and adding a new Key Activity to her team model (green sticky notes on the facing page). She recruited new Key Partners from other ThyssenKrupp divisions to help design and deliver the new training. Her new Customers helped co-create the training, as shown in the Customer Relationships building block.

Aligning her training team model with the Elevator Innovation Center model enabled Beatriz to demonstrate her team's value and secure a bigger budget. It also raised her profile within ThyssenKrupp as someone whose vision extends beyond the boundaries of a single job description.

"This two-level analysis forced us to examine alignment with a key internal Customer, not simply brainstorm new ideas," says Beatriz. "It was challenging but ultimately far more rewarding."

Lessons Beatriz Learned

- "In technical environments with many employees, work can become highly fractionated. Fractionation can make simple, overarching misalignments surprisingly easy to overlook."
- "Avoid using the Canvas to explain things to people untrained in Canvas use—it may confuse them. Give them some 'how-to' business model training first."
- "Everyone learns a lot when people from different teams help diagram a model."

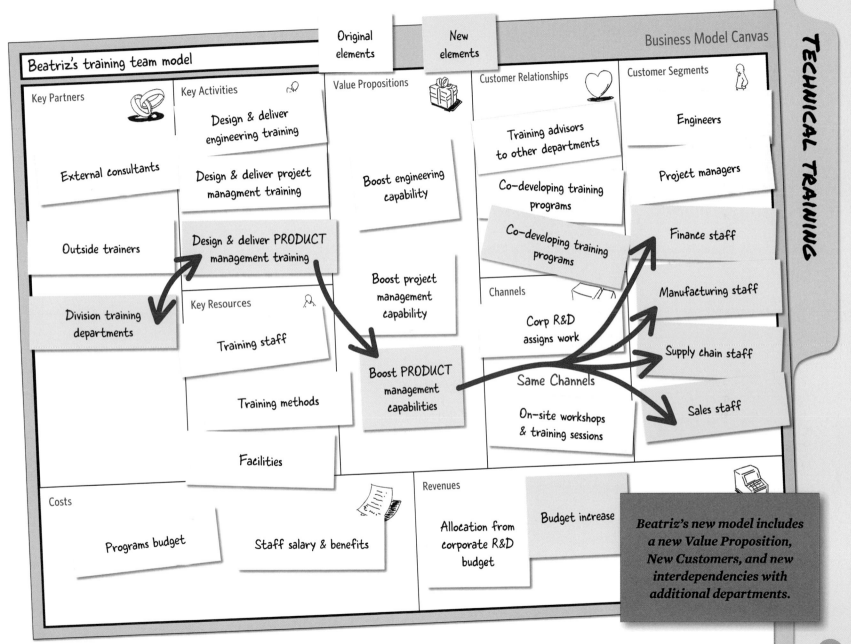

Business Model Canvas

Original elements

New elements

Beatriz's training team model

Key Partners 🔗

External consultants

Outside trainers

Division training departments

Key Activities

Design & deliver engineering training

Design & deliver project managment training

Design & deliver PRODUCT management training

Key Resources

Training staff

Training methods

Facilities

Value Propositions 🎁

Boost engineering capability

Boost project management capability

Boost PRODUCT management capabilities

Customer Relationships ♥

Training advisors to other departments

Co-developing training programs

Co-developing training programs

Channels

Corp R&D assigns work

Same Channels

On-site workshops & training sessions

Customer Segments 👶

Engineers

Project managers

Finance staff

Manufacturing staff

Supply chain staff

Sales staff

Costs

Programs budget

Staff salary & benefits

Revenues

Allocation from corporate R&D budget

Budget increase

Beatriz's new model includes a new Value Proposition, New Customers, and new interdependencies with additional departments.

The Alignment Canvas

Beatriz juxtaposed her training team model on the Innovation Center's model to learn how she could better align her work with Customer goals. You can do the same with the Alignment Canvas.

The Alignment Canvas shows two related business models on the same sheet: a lower-level (less complex) business model and a higher-level (more complex) business model. The higher and lower models can be related through hierarchy, an interdependency, subsidiary status, Customer-provider status, or a combination of these. Similar to how the Modello restaurant is a Customer of the kitchen team, the Elevator Innovation Center is a Customer of Beatriz's team.

The terms "lower" and "higher" refer only to complexity or level in a hierarchy—they do not indicate a judgment or value. On an Alignment Canvas, the higher-level model takes precedence over the lower-level model: usually the lower-level model is modified or adjusted to meet the needs of the higher-level model. Take a look at the Alignment Canvas on the facing page.

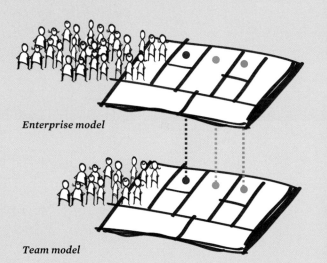

Enterprise model

Team model

Key Partners

List parties who either 1) provide us with a Key Resource, or 2) perform a Key Activity on our behalf.

List parties who 1) provide you with a Key Resource, or 2) perform a Key Activity on your behalf.

Costs

List the biggest Costs incurred for Key Resources, Key Activities, and Key Partners.

Higher Model:

Lower Model:

Key Activities

Describe essential ongoing actions that create, communicate, facilitate evaluation of, sell, deliver, or support our Value Proposition(s).

Describe essential ongoing actions whereby you create, communicate, facilitate evaluation of, sell, deliver, or support our Value Proposition(s).

Key Resources

List the most important resources (people, financial, intellectual, physical) we need to create, communicate, sell, deliver, and support our Value Proposition(s).

List the most important resources (interests, personality, skills & abilities, experience, knowledge, etc.) you have to create, communicate, sell, deliver, and support the team's Value Proposition(s).

Value Propositions

Describe Customer problems we solve (Jobs-to-be-Done), benefits we deliver, and/or Customer needs we satisfy. Include service/product names.

Describe Customer problems you solve, benefits you deliver, and/or Customer needs you satisfy.

Customer Relationships

Describe the nature of the relationships we have to
1) provide post-purchase Customer support, and
2) introduce Customers to other offers.

Describe the nature of the relationships you have to
1) provide post-purchase Customer support, and 2) introduce Customers to other offers.

Channels

List key prospective Customer touchpoints that 1) create awareness,
2) enable evaluation,
3) enable purchase, and/or
4) deliver Value.

List key prospective Customer touchpoints through which you 1) create awareness,
2) enable evaluation, 3) enable purchase, and/or 4) deliver Value.

Customer Segments

List in priority order the most important Customer segments to whom we deliver Value.

List in priority order the most important internal or external Customer segments to whom you deliver Value.

Revenue & Rewards

Describe the specific form of Revenue and/or Reward provided by each Customer segment.

List the biggest costs (financial, emotional, social, financial, etc.) of doing your work.

Describe Revenue or Rewards (financial, emotional, social, personal, etc.) you receive from Customers.

Using the Alignment Canvas

To use the Alignment Canvas, start with two related business models. Draw the higher-level model in the upper, unshaded portion of each building block. Then, draw the lower business model in the lower, shaded portion of each building block (room for posting elements is limited, so being concise is important).

The Alignment Canvas on the facing page shows Modello (the higher-level model) in blue sticky notes and shows the dining room team (the lower-level model) in yellow sticky notes.

Next, compare the upper and lower models. You might start by asking two questions: *What are the areas of greatest similarity between these two models?* and *What are the areas of greatest difference?*

In the Alignment Canvas on the facing page, you can see that the Modello restaurant serves three Customer segments, identified by number in priority order: 1) dinner crowd, 2) lunch crowd, and 3) private parties. The dining room team serves three Customer segments, also identified by number in priority order: 1) Modello, 2) dinner crowd, and 3) lunch crowd.

Juxtaposing the two models on the Alignment Canvas reveals a key difference: the dining room team does not serve the restaurant's third customer segment, private parties. The Channel Modello uses to reach that customer segment is *catering*. The catering Channel is missing from the dining room team's business model.

That was about to change, thanks to a situation-savvy server named Dennis.

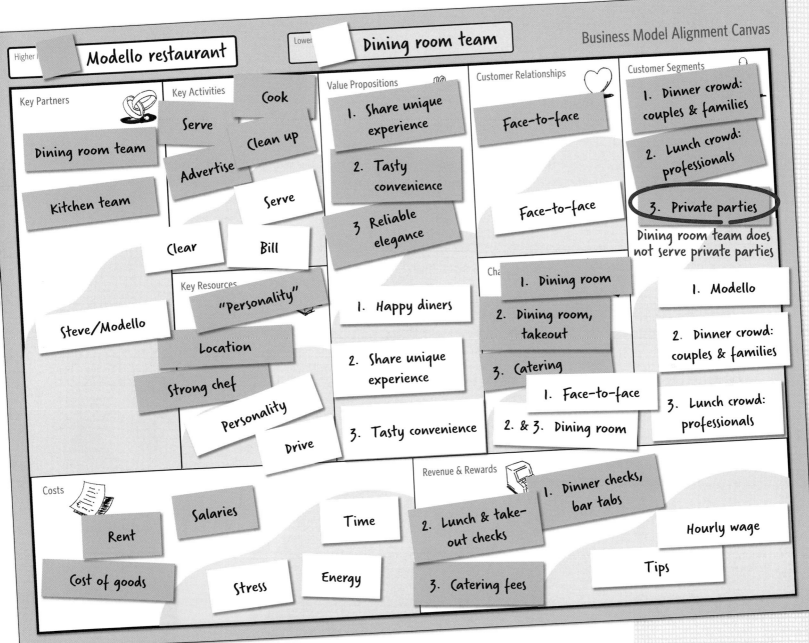

Modello restaurant

Key Partners

Dining room team

Kitchen team

Steve/Modello

Key Activities

Cook

Serve

Clean up

Advertise

Serve

Clear

Bill

Key Resources

"Personality"

Location

Strong chef

Personality

Drive

Value Propositions

1. Share unique experience
2. Tasty convenience
3. Reliable elegance

1. Happy diners
2. Share unique experience
3. Tasty convenience

Customer Relationships

Face-to-face

Face-to-face

Channels

1. Dining room
2. Dining room, takeout
3. Catering

1. Face-to-face
2. & 3. Dining room

Customer Segments

1. Dinner crowd: couples & families
2. Lunch crowd: professionals
3. Private parties

Dining room team does not serve private parties

1. Modello
2. Dinner crowd: couples & families
3. Lunch crowd: professionals

Costs

Rent

Salaries

Cost of goods

Stress

Time

Energy

Revenue & Rewards

1. Dinner checks, bar tabs
2. Lunch & take-out checks
3. Catering fees

Hourly wage

Tips

Dennis's Accidental Discovery

Dennis is one of Modello's top servers. He works four shifts a week in the restaurant and sometimes acts as headwaiter for private parties Modello caters. Thanks to his naturally friendly demeanor, Dennis knows a number of regular customers by name. One lunch regular, Phil, is a sales director for a pharmaceutical manufacturer.

While serving Phil and a companion one day, Dennis was surprised to hear the two heatedly discussing food delivery services. Dennis was even more surprised when Phil asked him for his professional opinion regarding a good local caterer. "Well, our catering service makes everything on Modello's lunch menu available at off-site locations," Dennis replied. Dennis quickly forgot the exchange. But later that week, Phil's secretary called Steve and booked a catered luncheon for 15 people.

The following day, Steve took Dennis aside. "Phil booked us for a 15-person luncheon at Children's Orthopedic," he said. "Thanks for mentioning our catering. I wouldn't have guessed two sales reps would need more than that day's lunch."

Dennis shrugged. "He and that sales guy seemed pretty worked up over some sort of food delivery problem."

Steve, seemingly lost in thought, suddenly snapped to attention. "Buddy, you just gave me an idea about our business model!"

At the next all-staff meeting, Steve presented the Alignment Canvas from the previous page and made an announcement.

"You all know about our catering service, and some of you help with it. But when Dennis brought in a new catering client the other week, it became clear we can be more intentional about growing this part of our business." Steve gestured at the "private parties" sticky note on the Alignment Canvas, then continued. "From now on, any time one of your referrals results in a catering engagement, 8 precent of the bill—off the top—will go into the tip pool."

An enthusiastic murmur rippled through the room. Steve placed five new pink sticky notes on the Alignment Canvas as he spoke again. "Start thinking of private parties as one of your

Customer segments, and make 'mention catering' a Key Activity. But keep it low-key and context-appropriate. Not everyone needs food delivered!" The meeting broke up amid laughter among the staff, and Steve and Dennis walked together toward the dining room. "Now it's time for a talk with Phil," said Steve. "It's PINT time."

Dennis looked confused. "You're going to ask him out for a beer?"

Steve laughed. "Yup. We're going to talk about Problems, Issues, Needs, and Trends—over a pint!"

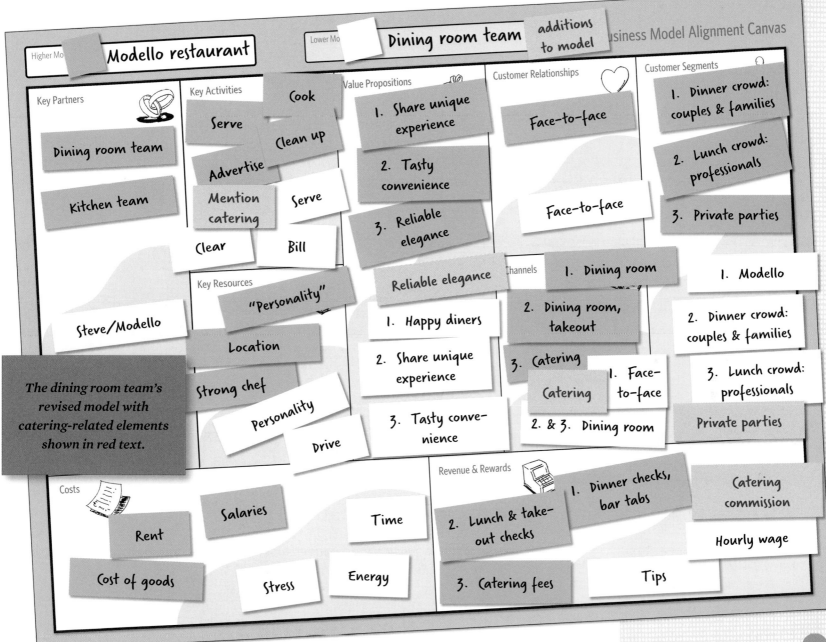

Modello restaurant

Dining room team — additions to model

Business Model Alignment Canvas

Higher Mo...

Lower Mo...

Key Partners

Dining room team

Kitchen team

Steve/Modello

Key Activities

Cook

Serve

Clean up

Advertise

Mention catering

Serve

Clear

Bill

Key Resources

"Personality"

Location

Strong chef

Personality

Drive

Value Propositions

1. Share unique experience
2. Tasty convenience
3. Reliable elegance

Reliable elegance

1. Happy diners
2. Share unique experience
3. Tasty convenience

Customer Relationships

Face-to-face

Face-to-face

Channels

1. Dining room
2. Dining room, takeout
3. Catering

Catering

1. Face-to-face

2. & 3. Dining room

Customer Segments

1. Dinner crowd: couples & families
2. Lunch crowd: professionals
3. Private parties

1. Modello
2. Dinner crowd: couples & families
3. Lunch crowd: professionals

Private parties

Costs

Salaries

Rent

Cost of goods

Time

Stress

Energy

Revenue & Rewards

1. Dinner checks, bar tabs
2. Lunch & take-out checks
3. Catering fees

Catering commission

Hourly wage

Tips

The dining room team's revised model with catering-related elements shown in red text.

A Pharmaceutical Industry **PINT** (Problems, Issues, Needs, and Trends)

"Thanks for taking the time to see me, Phil," said Steve, raising a pint of stout and clinking glasses with the pharmaceutical executive. "No doubt you're crazy busy."

"Always happy to help an entrepreneur, Steve," Phil replied, draining a full quarter of his drink in one swallow. "What can I do for you?"

Steve pulled a notebook from his bag. "I'm so glad the Children's Orthopedic luncheon went well. I'm curious—why did you need to arrange food when the hospital has its own cafeteria?"

Phil shook his head as though he could hardly believe his own response to the question. "In the drug sales game, we can't go into hospitals and clinics like we used to," he said. "Industry guidelines now say all our demos and pitches have to be made outside of treatment hours. That makes lunch the only practical time to meet medical staff. So the only way to get them together is to offer a nice free meal."

Steve was scribbling furiously in his notebook. Phil peered over the top of his glass. "What's that orange and blue diagram?"

"It's a way to analyze **P**roblems, **I**ssues, **N**eeds, and **T**rends," Steve replied. He turned his notebook around so Phil could see the **P-I-N-T** acronym laid out in four orange boxes. He gestured toward the **T** box. "It sounds like on-site meal hosting is a growing trend."

"You wouldn't believe it," said Phil. "My salespeople spend hours searching online or calling caterers. That's not a good use of their time." He drained his glass and signaled the waiter for another round.

"Let me see if I've got this straight," said Steve. He pointed toward the lines he had written in three of the orange boxes. "The pharmaceutical industry **T**rend toward on-site lunchtime presentations created a **P**roblem: salespeople spend too much time arranging meals. That in turn created a **N**eed for reliable catering. Does that sound right?"

"You've got it," said Phil, accepting a fresh glass of stout from the waiter. "Let's raise a pint to your **PINT** analysis!" The two men laughed.

Who You Help

Problem or **P**otential
Sales reps spend too much time arranging meals

Issue

Needs
Reliable local catering with good food, easy to arrange

Trend
Industry guidelines mean reps have to demo during lunch

SIRP (Solutions, Innovation, Resources, or Positioning Ideas)

"Let me share how it works," Steve offered. "First, you fill in the **PINT** elements like this. Do these look right to you?" He pointed at the orange boxes.

Phil nodded and took a long draw on his stout.

Steve used his pen to point at the blue boxes in the diagram. "Next, you think of what **S**olutions, **I**nnovation, **R**esources, or **P**ositioning ideas effectively address the key **PINT** elements," he continued. "In your case, it's clear that your salespeople need caterers who understand their need for last-minute arrangements. Maybe it would help if they could order online at any hour, even if the restaurant was closed?"

Phil nodded his head vigorously, and Steve wrote the words in the **S** box.

"Great stuff, Steve," said Phil, replacing his glass on the table. "Let me know if you ever get tired of the restaurant business—we could use a guy like you in my unit!"

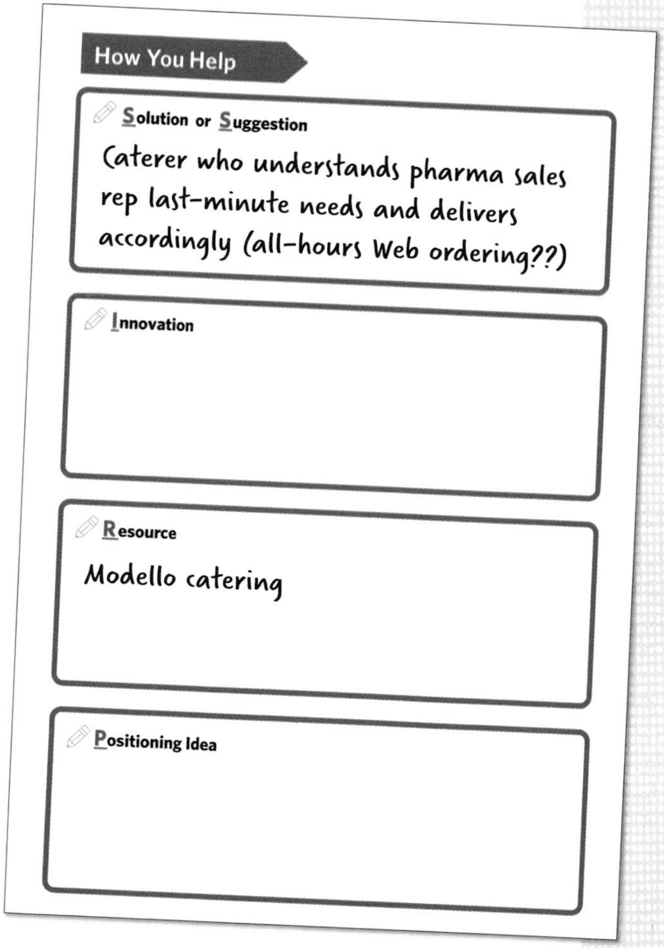

How You Help

Solution or **S**uggestion

Caterer who understands pharma sales rep last-minute needs and delivers accordingly (all-hours Web ordering??)

Innovation

Resource

Modello catering

Positioning Idea

The Valuable Work Detector

Steve had learned the **PINT** acronym from Sally, a friend who had enrolled in an evening MBA program while working full-time for a medical device manufacturer. It was part of a tool Sally called the ***Valuable Work Detector***.

Steve remembered discussing a simple but profound issue with Sally: *What creates work?* Few people think seriously about this question, she had said. Yet many people assume that work somehow grows out of having a "job" with a title such as *accountant, logistics manager,* or *marketing assistant.*

This tacit "jobs equals work" assumption spells trouble for leaders, said Sally, because it means people 1) *define* work as a *job description* and 2) *confine* work to *activities proscribed by their job titles.* The job-equals-work assumption limits self-direction and engagement. *People need a bigger theory of work,* Sally had insisted.

The Valuable Work Detector is based on the commonsense idea that work is generated by four things common to all organizations: Problems or Potentials, Issues, Needs, or Trends

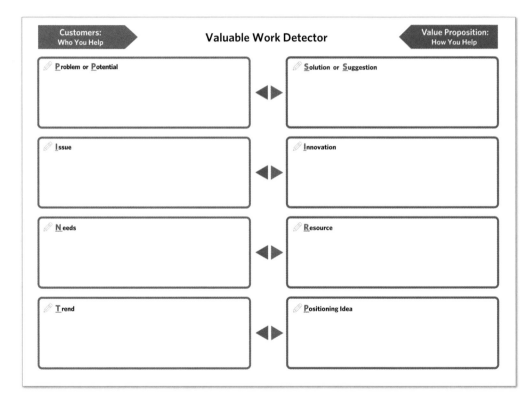

(**PINT** elements). Each **PINT** element can become a source of worthwhile work. Each element serves as a lens for detecting work-that-needs-doing, *before* the work has been addressed by a service, product, internal action, or a new job position.

The **PINT** Elements

Sally illustrated each of the four **PINT** elements using examples from her own experience working as part of a human resources team:

1. Problem or Potential
Something is broken or not working well, or an opportunity exists for something new. For example, employee turnover at Sally's company was too high.

2. Issue
Nothing is broken, but rules, regulations, or conditions are changing. For example, upcoming legislation seemed certain to change how Sally's company could employ foreign graduate students as interns or contract workers.

3. Need
Something is missing, or there is a desire for something new or different. For example, Sally's employer planned to enter South America and needed talented employees with Spanish and Portuguese language and cultural skills.

4. Trend
Things are changing or moving in new directions, or people are behaving differently. For example, the growing use of robotics in medicine suggested that Sally's firm needed engineers with robotics expertise.

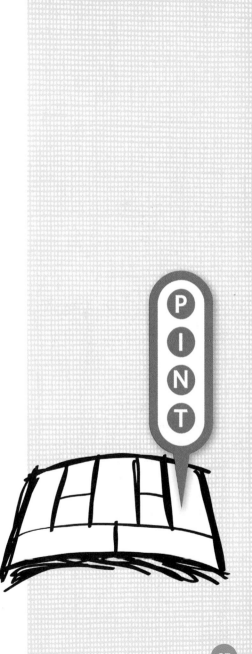

Using the Valuable Work Detector
The first step is to pick a key Customer your team serves and consider a ***Problem or Potential, Issue, Need,*** or ***Trend*** the Customer faces. Identify one or two elements that seem important, and write a brief, concise description of each. Think of the four PINT elements as residing in the Customer building block of a Canvas.

If you have direct knowledge of a Customer ***Problem or Potential, Issue, Need,*** or ***Trend,*** your description represents fact. Otherwise, your description represents a hypothesis you should test with your Customer or a knowledgeable insider.

The **SIRP** Elements

After identifying one or more valid **PINT** elements, explain how your team might respond. A response is a potential Value Proposition that addresses the identified **PINT** elements. This Value Proposition could include any of four elements represented by the acronym **SIRP**:

1. Solution or Suggestion

*A fix, repair, or suggestion for new method, service, or product that addresses a **Problem or Potential**.* For example, Sally's human resources team implemented flexible scheduling after exit interview analysis showed key employees had left to seek more accommodating working hours.

2. Innovation

*Proactively adapting things or circumstances to address an **Issue**.* For example, Sally's team attended several academic events and learned about two promising new domestic graduate engineering programs. They then modified their recruitment targets to reduce dependence on engineers trained overseas.

3. Resource

*People, money, materials, or intellectual property that satisfies a **Need**.* For example, Sally's team solicited employee volunteers to respond to a survey about language skills, then recruited internally for new positions related to South American markets.

4. Positioning Idea

*A proposed way to exploit a **Trend** or minimize risk.* For example, Sally's team proposed endowing a robotics engineering professorship at a local graduate school.

Sally's team addressed all four **PINT** elements *without creating any new job titles or positions.*

Based on their **PINT** analysis, team members simply expanded their definition of what needed to be done, then did it—whether it fell under a "job description" or not. Note that the Valuable Work Detector can be used with both internal and external Customers.

Now it is your turn. Use the Valuable Work Detector on the facing page to detect some valuable work that one of *your* Customers needs done (you can also get free PDF versions of all the tools in this book by signing up at BusinessModelsForTeams.com).

Valuable Work Detector

✎ **P**roblem or **P**otential

Something is broken or not working well, or opportunity exists for something new.

✎ **S**olution or **S**uggestion

Fixes or repairs, or suggestions for new methods, services, or products.

✎ **I**ssue

Nothing is broken, but rules, regulations, or conditions are changing.

✎ **I**nnovation

Proactively adapting things or circumstances to address issues.

✎ **N**eeds

Something is missing, or there is a desire or appetite for something new or different.

✎ **R**esource

People, money, materials, or intellectual property that satisfy the need or desire.

✎ **T**rend

Things are changing or moving in new directions, or people are behaving differently.

✎ **P**ositioning Idea

Proposed ways to exploit trends or minimize risk.

Things to Try on Monday Morning

Draft Your Teamwork Table

First, try creating a teamwork table for a group you lead or support. Here is a template:

Role	Tasks	Customer	Result of task success	Consequence of task failure

Draft an Alignment Canvas

Second, grab some sticky notes and try diagramming your team and higher business models on an Alignment Canvas.

Use the completed canvas to see things you can:

1. Fix or improve
2. Eliminate (do less)
3. Reinforce (do more)
4. Realign
5. Take advantage of.

Key Partners

List parties who either
1) provide us with a Key Resource, or
2) perform a Key Activity on our behalf.

List parties who
1) provide you with a Key Resource, or
2) perform a Key Activity on your behalf.

Key Activities

Describe essential ongoing actions that create, communicate, facilitate evaluation of, sell, deliver, or support our Value Proposition(s).

Describe essential ongoing actions whereby you create, communicate, facilitate evaluation of, sell, deliver, or support our Value Proposition(s).

Key Resources

List the most important resources (people, financial, intellectual, physical) we need to create, communicate, sell, deliver, and support our Value Proposition(s).

List the most important resources (interests, personality, skills & abilities, experience, knowledge, etc.) you have to create, communicate, sell, deliver, and support the team's Value Proposition(s).

Costs

List the biggest Costs incurred for Key Resources, Key Activities, and Key Partners.

Higher Model:

Lower Model:

Value Propositions

Describe Customer problems we solve (Jobs-to-be-Done), benefits we deliver, and/or Customer needs we satisfy. Include service/product names.

Describe Customer problems you solve, benefits you deliver, and/or Customer needs you satisfy.

Customer Relationships

Describe the nature of the relationships we have to 1) provide post-purchase Customer support, and 2) introduce Customers to other offers.

Describe the nature of the relationships you have to 1) provide post-purchase Customer support, and 2) introduce Customers to other offers.

Channels

List key prospective Customer touchpoints that 1) create awareness, 2) enable evaluation, 3) enable purchase, and/or 4) deliver Value.

List key prospective Customer touchpoints through which you 1) create awareness, 2) enable evaluation, 3) enable purchase, and/or 4) deliver Value.

Customer Segments

List in priority order the most important Customer segments to whom we deliver Value.

List in priority order the most important internal or external Customer segments to whom you deliver Value.

Revenue & Rewards

Describe the specific form of Revenue and/or Reward provided by each Customer segment.

List the biggest costs (financial, emotional, social, financial, etc.) of doing your work.

Describe Revenue or Rewards (financial, emotional, social, personal, etc.) you receive from Customers.

Everyone Deserves a Room With a View

Most organizations attempt strategic planning in some form. They compose mission or vision statements, create strategy documents, or build five-year plans.

That is when the real challenge starts: how to socialize the strategy beyond the small, select group that devised it?

This pivotal task truly tests leadership's ability to explain and teach. What seems brilliant to strategy-makers often confuses the rest of the organization, who usually lack training or experience in market analysis, strategic planning, or organizational design. As a result, people return to over-focusing on what feels clear and familiar: the tasks in their job descriptions.

To get people to understand and follow a strategy, it must 1) be explained in easily understood terms, and 2) guide actual behavior.

Think of organizational and team business models as ideal windows that give everyone a "room with a view"—an unobstructed picture of how the organization works, and where people fit in.

The final step in achieving this is to define personal business models, the subject of the next chapter.

Chapter 4

Modeling People

Enterprises, Teams, and Individuals

By now you have seen how useful it is to view teams as having business models that complement enterprise models. Similarly, every individual has a *personal* business model that shows how they contribute to a team.

A personal model frames the true purpose of a person's work as a Value Proposition. When every person's personal model is in sync with team goals, you will lead an unbeatable group. On the other hand, when people are out of sync with their team, adjustments will be needed. As a leader who moves back and forth between personal needs and group goals, your job is to find misalignments and take action.

The purpose of this chapter is 1) to teach you how to use the Personal Business Model Canvas to draw and use personal business models, and 2) to show ways to identify misalignments between individuals and teams. The Personal Business Model Canvas uses the same enterprise business model vocabulary to frame individual work in terms of team and organizational goals. At the same time, it allows people to express their individuality and pursue personal ambitions in the most appropriate organizational role.

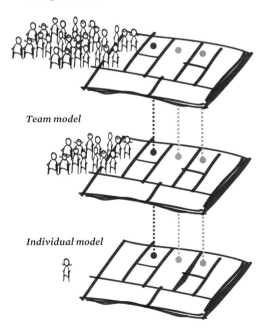

Enterprise model

Team model

Individual model

Personal Business Models

First, note some differences between group and personal models:

- In a personal business model, the Key Resource is *you*: your interests, skills and abilities, personality, and values. Compared to an enterprise or team, an individual is "resource-constrained"— another reason to recognize how much we depend on others to succeed.

- Unlike teams or enterprises that may deliver products to external Customers through their models, it is helpful to think of individuals as providing their labor as a *service*. That service is most often provided to internal Customers.

- A personal business model takes into account unquantifiable "soft" costs (such as stress) and "soft" rewards (such as professional growth). Most enterprise models consider only monetary costs and benefits.

Be sure to practice drawing your own personal business model before using personal business models with colleagues.[1]

The Building Blocks of a Personal Business Model

Here is an overview of each of the nine building blocks in a Personal Business Model Canvas. The building blocks are the same as for the team and enterprise Canvases, but alternate labels are provided to help people understand the language of business models in a personal way. The following building block descriptions assume *you* are using the personal Canvas to describe your own model.

Who You Are/What You Have (Key Resources)

This block defines several core assets: 1) your interests and what you consider important, 2) your skills and abilities, 3) your personality, and 4) your professional identity. Your interests—the things that excite you—may well be your most precious resource. As a leader, this is a good opportunity to assess your fit with your current role. Are your personal interests in line with team and enterprise aims? Be sure they are before asking others to follow your example!

What You Do (Key Activities)

What you do—your Key Activities—arise from who you are. In short, they are "driven" by your Key Resources. Professions usually have a recognizable constellation of Key Activities. Most university professors, for example, teach, do research, and provide some type of community service. Describe your Key Activities using action words (verbs) such as *sell, assemble,* or *recruit.*

A combination of several activities is usually required to create Value, but Customers rarely believe activity is valuable on its own. *Remember that Key Activities differ from Value.* Drawing personal business models will help you and your team distinguish Key Activities from Value.

Whom You Help (Customers)

As with the enterprise model, your most important Customer is the person who decides to pay for your services. But you may have other Customers as well, and naming them can be challenging. Internal Customers could include your boss, other leaders, your own employees, or certain Key Partners. External Customers are easier to recognize. Remember that external Customers pay for value, or receive value at no cost and are subsidized by paying Customers, taxpayers, or donors. But in most organizations, few workers have direct contact with external Customers, so they may be only weakly aware that external Customers ultimately pay for almost everything. A good way to build cost-consciousness and earnings-awareness is to have people draw personal business models that show both internal Customers and external Customers—the ones who really pay the bills.

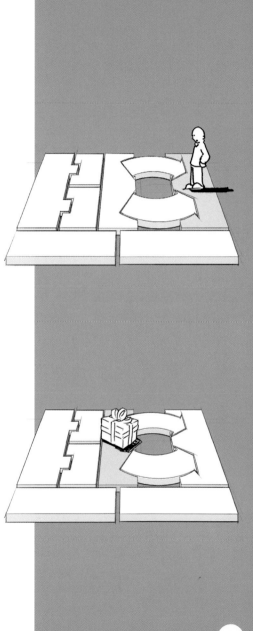

How You Help (Value Proposition)[2]

This is the heart of your personal business model. Your personal Value Proposition describes why your work matters to your Customer. It defines benefits delivered rather than activities performed. For example, a homeowner wanting to install a new fence needs a series of holes in specific places—she cares little about the digging itself. So, a laborer's Value Proposition is not "digging." Rather, it is "creating holes where and when the homeowner needs them." Your personal Value Proposition forms the core of your professional identity, which is discussed later in this chapter.

A good way to find your personal Value Proposition is to answer the question, *What job is my Customer 'hiring' me to perform? What does my Customer gain as a result of completing that job?*[3] Remember that benefits are often intangible. Examples may include *reduced risk, confidence in decisions, enhanced reputation, lower costs, attracting clients,* and so forth. Value Proposition and Customers are the two most important parts of your personal business model. Define Value Proposition and Customers, and you are mostly done—drawing the rest of your model will be straightforward. Just be sure your personal Value Proposition fits with your team and your organization's goals!

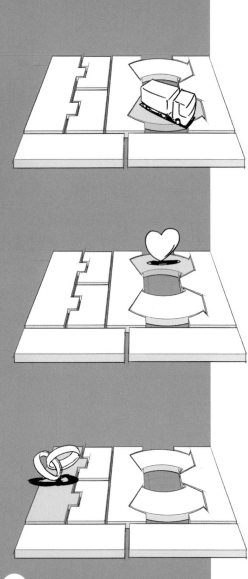

More Personal Business Model Building Blocks

How They Know You/How You Deliver (Channels)

What we refer to as Channels is really the marketing process: 1) creating awareness, 2) inducing evaluation, 3) selling, 4) delivery, and 5) post-sale follow-up (which takes place in the Customer Relationships building block). Most people think of Channels in terms of delivery. You might deliver your work via written reports; talking to people; uploading code to a server; driving a vehicle; or in many other ways. But guard against an excessive focus on the delivery and follow-up Channel phases. Longtime employees of the same organization often find themselves in an endless loop of work delivery and follow-up and fail to "market" themselves internally by creating awareness of their value elsewhere in the organization.

How You Interact (Customer Relationships)

A good vendor who acquires a Customer follows up after delivery to make sure the Customer is satisfied. Follow-up can take the form of face-to-face discussions; e-mail/telephone/video/chat; written reports; personal inspections; wiki, blog, or Intranet or Internet postings, and so forth. This is an opportunity for people to inform new colleagues of the help they can offer. For those who work primarily with internal Customers, this is another opportunity to recognize and strengthen links within the team or enterprise.

Who Helps You (Key Partners)

When working in teams, this is the go-to place for help. Key Partners can include teammates, your leader or supervisor, direct reports, suppliers or external partners, peers in different parts of the organization, industry colleagues, or even external Customers (remember that a single party, such as a Customer, can appear in more than one building block within a business model). Key Partners can also be truly personal: they might include your spouse, other family members, personal or spiritual mentors, or good friends. Leaders often gain much by encouraging people to bring their whole selves to work rather than struggling to maintain a narrow, strictly professional "face." This is especially so when leaders model such behavior themselves.[4]

Rewards (Revenue)

Rewards include "hard" compensation such as salary, fees, stock options, royalties, bonuses, or other cash-equivalent payments. "Hard" benefits include health insurance, retirement packages, childcare leave, tuition assistance, and so forth. "Soft" benefits include development, recognition, social contribution, fellowship, sense of belonging, flexible working hours or schedule, and so forth.

People often value soft rewards over hard rewards, so a leader's job may include setting or negotiating appropriate rewards. Look for opportunities to create soft rewards that directly address the four intrinsic human motivators.

Intrinsic Human Motivator	Soft Reward
Purpose	Social contribution, helping others
Autonomy	Flexible schedule or location, authority to determine *what* as well as *how* of work
Relatedness	Recognition, sense of community, permission to bring whole self to work
Mastery	Learning, professional development

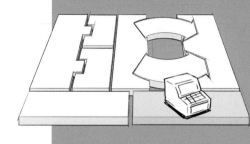

Investments (Costs)

People invest significant time and energy in their work—and sometimes pay the price in the form of stress. Other investments might include commuting or travel time, unpaid overtime or expectations to respond to work-related issues after hours, and unreimbursed expenses for training, tools, or clothing.

People often say there are two currencies in life: time and money. We believe there is a third currency: *flexibility*. Schedule or location flexibility may be sacrificed (become a Cost) or gained (become a Reward). Avoid underestimating how important flexibility can be—sometimes it is more important than compensation!

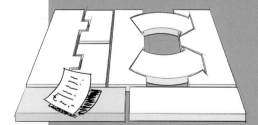

The Personal Business Model Canvas

Here is a complete Personal Business Model Canvas, along with "hint" questions to help you fill in each building block. Why not grab some sticky notes and try drawing your own personal business model right now?

Who Helps You
(Key Partners)

- Who helps you provide Value to others?
- Who supports you in other ways, and how?
- Does anyone supply Key Resources or perform Key Activities on your behalf?
- Could someone do so?

Key Partners could include:
· Friends
· Family members
· Supervisors
· Human resource personnel
· Coworkers
· Suppliers
· Professional association members
· Mentors or counselors, etc.

What You Do
(Key Activities)

- List several critical activities you perform at work each day that distinguish your occupation from others.
- Which of these Key Activities does your Value Proposition require?
- Which activities do your Channels and Customer Relationships require?

Consider how your activities may be grouped in the following areas:
· Making (building, creating, solving, delivering, etc.)
· Selling (informing, persuading, teaching, etc.)
· Supporting (administering, calculating, organizing, etc.)

Who You Are/What You Have
(Key Resources)

- What do you get most excited about at work?
- Rank your preferences: Do you like dealing primarily with
  1) people, 2) information/ideas, or
  3) physical objects/outdoor work?
- Describe a couple of your abilities (things you do naturally without effort) and a few of your skills (things you have learned to do).
- List some of your other resources: personal network, reputation, experience, physical capabilities, etc.

Investments (Costs)

- What do you give to your work (time, energy, etc.)?
- What do you give up in order to work (family or personal time, etc.)?
- Which Key Activities are most "expensive" (draining, stressful, etc.)?

List soft and hard costs associated with your work:

Soft costs:
· Stress or dissatisfaction
· Lack of personal or professional growth opportunities
· Low recognition or lack of social contribution
· Lack of flexibility, excessive availability expectations

Hard costs:
· Excessive time or travel commitments
· Unreimbursed commuting or travel expenses
· Unreimbursed training, education, tool, materials, or other costs

How You Help
(Value Propositions)

- What Value do you deliver to Customers?
- What problem do you solve or need do you satisfy?
- Describe specific benefits Customers enjoy as a result of your work.

Consider whether the help you provide:
· Reduces risk
· Lowers costs
· Increases convenience or usability
· Improves performance
· Increases enjoyment or fulfills a basic need
· Fulfills a social need (brand, status, approval, etc.)
· Satisfies an emotional need

How You Interact
(Customer Relationships)

Channel Phase 5. Followup: How do you continue to support Customers and ensure they are satisfied?
- What kinds of relationships do your Customers expect you to establish and maintain with them?
- Describe the types of relationships you have in place now.

Examples might include:
· Face-to-face personal assistance
· Remote help via telephone, e-mail, chat, Skype, etc.
· Colleague or user communities
· Co-creation
· Self-service or automated services

How They Know You/
How You Deliver (Channels)

- Through which Channels do your Customers want to be reached?
- How are you reaching them now?
- Which Channels work best?

Channel Phases:
1. Awareness: How do potential Customers find out about you?
2. Evaluation: How do you help potential Customers appraise your Value?
3. Purchase: How do new Customers hire you or buy your services?
4. Delivery: How do you deliver Value to Customers?

Who You Help
(Customer)

- For whom do you create Value?
- Who is your most important Customer?
- Who depends on your work in order to get their own jobs done?
- Who are your Customers' Customers?

Rewards (Revenue)

- For what Value are your Customers truly willing to pay?
- For what do they pay now?
- How do they pay now?
- How might they prefer to pay?

Describe your Rewards

Hard benefits might include:
· Salary
· Wages or professional fees
· Health and disability insurance
· Retirement benefits
· Stock options or profit-sharing plans
· Tuition assistance, transportation or child care allowances, etc.

Soft benefits might include:
· Satisfaction, enjoyment
· Professional development
· Recognition
· Sense of community
· Social contribution
· Flexible hours or conditions

A Personal Business Model Example

Sean Backus was an outstanding new graduate who joined programming teams at two companies in succession—and leaders let him quit each time. Yet Sean's Value Proposition—solving business problems with software—was perfectly aligned with each company. Here is how Sean's personal business model appeared during his first two jobs:

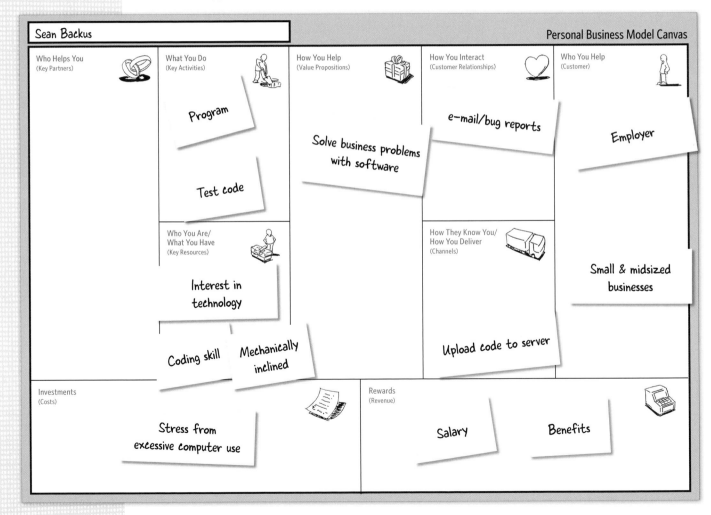

Sean Backus				Personal Business Model Canvas

Who Helps You (Key Partners)

What You Do (Key Activities)

Program

Test code

How You Help (Value Propositions)

Solve business problems with software

How You Interact (Customer Relationships)

e-mail/bug reports

Who You Help (Customer)

Employer

Who You Are/What You Have (Key Resources)

Interest in technology

Coding skill   Mechanically inclined

How They Know You/How You Deliver (Channels)

Upload code to server

Small & midsized businesses

Investments (Costs)

Stress from excessive computer use

Rewards (Revenue)

Salary   Benefits

A Happier Teammate, a Stronger Team

At his third job, Sean realized he had been neglecting his strong social tendencies. Programming-only roles had frustrated him, because the immediate work environment—solitary coding in cubicles—satisfied only his technology interests. Sean talked with his manager about his interest in instructing, and the two agreed he would start training other programmers in debugging techniques. Sean's satisfaction soared, thanks to a more varied and social workload, plus a newfound ability to pursue mastery, both for himself and other employees. He contributed even more in the new role, because fewer software bugs meant happier clients.

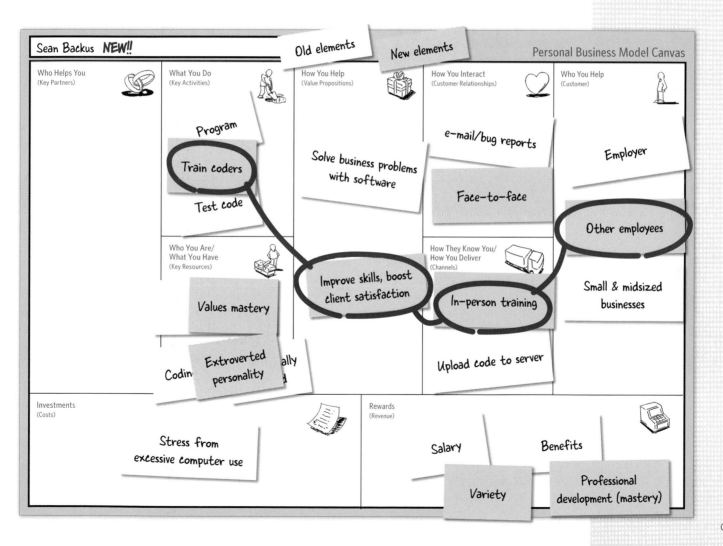

Strengthening Teams Using Professional Identity

A Leader's Tough Job

Leaders have a tough job. They must help people to either 1) better contribute to current teams, 2) move elsewhere in the organization where they can better contribute, or 3) move out of the organization when there is no longer a good fit. Determining fit with team or organization calls for thinking in terms of *roles* rather than *skills* (or "jobs"). For example, Sean's managers consistently thought of him only in terms of *skills:* they focused on tasks he could perform rather than roles he might play. Sean was indeed highly skilled, and his first two managers failed to notice when he seemed to become less engaged in his work. Fortunately for both Sean and his employer, his third manager grasped the concept of roles. To start thinking in terms of roles, here is a technique you can pair with business models.

Professional Identity

Sean over-identified as a programmer. But when he brought his extroverted personality and desire for mastery to work—something he had not done before—he and his manager created a new role for him as *someone who improves and assures code quality.* In this new role, Sean not only contributed more value, he started expressing his true *professional identity.*

Professional identity is the persistent occupational essence that, together with value delivery style, distinguishes one professional from another.

Think of your own professional identity as the benefits you consistently deliver to Customers as a one-person business model. That identity would remain even if you were stripped of all job titles, awards, college or university degrees, certificates, or licenses. Just as personality describes your psychological essence, professional identity describes your occupational essence. It includes your value delivery style. In Sean's case, it was a combination of casual, self-deprecating humor and nonchalant technical expertise that trainees found compelling and useful.

Helping others develop their professional identities is a good way to help them better contribute to a team—or find somewhere else to contribute. And helping others claim their professional identities is among the most satisfying things you can accomplish as a leader. To see why, consider the traditional way organizations recruited, promoted, and transferred people.

Traditional Needs-Resource Matching

Organizations traditionally recruited, promoted, and transferred people by *matching needs and resources*. Things that needed doing were considered "needs" and people were considered "resources." "Resource" was further defined in terms of *Knowledge, Skills, and Abilities* (KSAs). Job postings listed required KSAs, and someone with corresponding knowledge, skills, and abilities would be hired, promoted, or transferred.

Matching needs and resources by using KSAs certainly increases the chance that an individual will contribute to a team. But KSAs are an incomplete way of seeing people. Professional identity, on the other hand, expresses someone's talent, ability to get things done, and most important, Value Proposition. And syncing personal *Value Propositions* to team or enterprise goals is the essence of leadership.

Helping Team Members Define Professional Identity

How can you help team members with their professional identity? For starters, be clear about your organization's employee development policy. A growing number of progressive organizations have adopted the policy that it is not the organization's job to develop people. *Rather, people are given the opportunity to develop themselves by doing the work of the organization.*[5]

After clarifying your policy, consider the importance of feedback. Few people are naturally self-observant, so they need plenty of feedback. That is why creating feedback-rich environments—for yourself and for your colleagues—is a crucial leadership responsibility. Remember that you are the most important source of feedback for people who report directly to you. As teamwork consultant Patrick Lencioni puts it, other than spouses, no one does as much as a workplace leader to determine people's sense of professional self.[6] Taking a genuine personal interest in your teammates—and letting them bring their "whole selves" to work—is the single most important thing you can do to foster the kind of informal, ongoing feedback that is far more powerful than formal, infrequent professional development sessions.

Consider yourself both a feedback-giving and feedback-gathering tool. When you make the rounds and talk with colleagues and their Customers, you offer objective perspectives that help people reality-check their personal opinions. Internal surveys can help, too. You might ask a human resources professional to design a survey for your team members, or use an established method such as 360 Reach.[7]

Exercise: Define Your Professional Identity

Here is an exercise that helps colleagues define their professional identity. You can conduct this exercise when interviewing someone who is about to join or leave your team, during a formal development session, or simply as a break from the regular routine with colleagues you now lead or supervise. This four-step exercise is best completed in two sessions, with the quote-gathering and style description tasks assigned in Steps 1 and 2 as "homework" to be submitted in a separate session (mature or highly self-aware participants may be able to complete the exercise in a single session). The only requirement is paper, pencil, and a quiet place to hold the discussion—preferably in a cafeteria, coffee shop, or other place you do not usually meet with the person. Step 1 of the exercise can be conducted with a group as well. Begin with an assurance that this is not a performance review—it is a *performing* review!

Step 1. Define the Results You Produce

Ask three different people who know you well to briefly describe the results you produce at work. People to be quoted can include current or former Customers, partners, bosses, teammates, a coach, commanding officer, teacher, or cler-gyperson. Their quotes should describe results, not activities. Also, ask quote-givers to describe your work *style;* how you appear to others as you produce results. Aim to compile 150 to 250 words of feedback or observations and write them down on a sheet of paper. See the example of quotes compiled by Ellen, who worked in corporate communications for Boeing.

Step 2. Describe Your Style

Review the quotes carefully. Then, summarize the *style* the quote-givers suggest you display in producing results. Use key words from your quote collection, plus your own words. Write this summary on a separate sheet of paper or sticky note. Here is what Ellen wrote for Step 2:

Step 1. The results of Ellen's survey on environmental stewardship helped us change the environmental engagement program. She went beyond a few interviews with environmentally astute employees and used data, not just passion, to back up the ideas she wrote about.
(Director of Environmental Services)

When she organized the Design for Environment initiative during Engineer Week we had more volunteers than we could use. We actually had to turn people away. Clearly values environmental quality and protections and gets others engaged in these issues.
(Chief Engineer, Supplier Services Group)

Ellen initiated and then co-led the team that created a successful customer service recognition program, despite changes in direction from incoming executives and division reorganizations. Her diplomatic style enabled her to coax people along so that the program never got derailed.
(Corporate Communications Director)

Step 2. I engage others and generate enthusiasm. I shine light on others' work. Diplomatic. Resilient in the face of changing objectives. Do more than just meet standards.

If you assigned Steps 1 and 2 as homework, have the participant bring two copies of each of their documents to the next session. Give the Step 3 instruction, then read over the documents while the participant works on Step 3.

Step 3. Summarize Your Professional Identity

Summarize your quote compilation in a brief, first-person ("I") statement. This should be a concise summary of what you deliver—your Value Proposition—and the way your deliver it. Keep your statement to 50 words or fewer. Here is what Ellen wrote:

> Step 3. I intuitively uncover hidden stories that demand sharing.
>
> People feel pride and accomplishment when reading what I write about them.
>
> I'm a corporate diplomat who shuttles across organizational borders to produce strategic, sense-making stories.

Step 4. Debrief

Compare your colleague's compiled quotes from Step 1 with the Step 2 style description. Do they seem to be accurately capturing what other people said? Do they show good awareness of their value delivery style?

You may find some of the following debriefing questions helpful:

- Do you have a strength others noticed but in which you yourself lack interest?
- What do these quotes and descriptions suggest are key values you use to make judgements, choices, or decisions?
- What is an ideal but feasible work scenario in which you use and develop this professional identity?

A colleague's professional identity will evolve and change over time, often without that colleague realizing it. That is why it is important to start early and repeat this exercise periodically with direct reports or colleagues you supervise. You are gathering feedback about the manner in which people perform in various roles. We have all seen people who achieve solid results but leave a trail of conflict, discord, or disengagement in their wake. *How* people deliver results matters.

As with all leadership techniques, it is smart to practice on your own before helping others. Try the Define Your Professional Identity exercise together with a colleague or other thought partner.

Using Professional Identity to Help People Better Align with Teams

As a leader, you may have already discovered that developing professional identity pays far greater dividends than merely pursuing titles, position, or status. Helping colleagues pursue their professional identities will increase their engagement and help them achieve better fit with their teams. Here is an example:

Sarah, the managing director of an advertising agency, recognized Randy, an account manager, for his outstanding ability to deliver inspiring client presentations. But she also noticed Randy's tendency to over-entertain—and miss client cues that they were ready to hear quantitative justification for his creative ideas.

Sarah had Randy try the Define Your Professional Identity exercise. After Randy came up with the statement *Each encounter leaves them delighted and demystified,* Sarah prompted him to name two roles he frequently played. He came up with "entertainer" and "professor." She then coached him to recognize that "entertainer" was his dominant style, and that he needed to intentionally shift to "professor" mode when necessary. Using professional identity helped Sarah maintain a coaching role for herself and avoid micromanaging Randy's work.

Using Professional Identity to Align and Engage

Most people strive to bring their best and highest selves to work. Everyone has something special to offer beyond the basic skills or knowledge that brought them to your team. But many struggle to understand their talents beyond Knowledge, Skills, and Abilities: they need help converting them into a worthwhile Value Propositions. Having them draw personal business models is a good first step. Then, when colleagues define their professional identities, they are more likely to start consciously recognizing how their Value Propositions can address **Problems, Issues, Needs,** and **Trends.**

Keep in mind that inexperienced colleagues may lack sufficient accomplishments to describe their impact. Encourage them to be self-observant and notice even their small results—not merely their activities—and to ask for feedback from those they serve. In the next section, see how one leader used professional identity, not only to save his firm from losing a valuable colleague, but to jumpstart business development in an important new sector.

Guess who got hired?

A clarified professional identity often reveals new opportunities unconstrained by job categories. For example, during a job interview with a medical device manufacturer, Hitoshi Koba, an engineering PhD candidate researching robotic medical devices, abandoned his technology-focused self-description and spontaneously claimed his professional identity as a "warrior in the battle against arteriosclerosis." Interviewers were impressed: Mr. Koba's professional identity elevated him beyond the advertised "engineer" category and immediately aligned him with the employer's purpose. Guess who got hired?

Off Target

"Did I shoot myself in the foot by losing the GHS and state bids? I feel like I've lost my groove . . ." said Wayne. He looked worried.

Jim Thomas, Human Resources Director for transportation consultancy FLR, snapped to attention. He heard a mix of frustration, confession, and a cry for help in Wayne's statement—and immediately recognized that FLR might be in danger of losing a key colleague.

Wayne was a senior transportation engineer who had been poised for promotion to principal transportation engineer when two key bids were lost to FLR's competitors. Jim suspected that Wayne, while planning and preparing the bid presentations for clients, had deferred excessively to the project leader, who tended to rely on data-heavy PowerPoint slides. Frustrated and discouraged following the lost bids, Wayne had asked for a confidential conversation with the HR Director.

Wayne's identity within FLR was that of "firm nerd." Though not an information technology professional per se, Wayne had suggested many of the tools that improved the firm's use of cloud technology. Now, thought Jim, Wayne had lost perspective on his own contributions—and possibly on a promising new market. Jim asked Wayne to complete Part 1 of the Define Your Professional Identity exercise and return two days later for another confidential conference. At their second meeting, here is what Wayne presented for Define the Results You Produce:

> I notice trends buried in tons of data we collect. But I'm not a programmer or software geek—I make mysterious data seem friendly.
> I turn it into information that clients use to make decisions and solve real transportation problems.

Next, while Jim watched, Wayne wrote the following for Step 3: Summarize Your Professional Identity:

> Nerd who creates insights by telling stories with data.

Jim and Wayne discussed Wayne's statements, then turned their attention to decisions made at a recent strategic planning retreat. FLR management had foreseen that Google's computer-driven cars would come to cities sooner than expected, and that smart highways and ubiquitous embedded monitors would tell the moment-to-moment story of where people were and where they wanted to go. But preparing for all this would require tremendous amounts of engineering and data science work—work FLR was well-positioned to undertake.

At the retreat, therefore, FLR had modified its enterprise business model by formally adding a new Value Proposition (provide cities with cloud-based smart transportation grids that can double the people-moving capacity of existing infrastructure), a new Key Resource (big data analysis capability), a new Key Activity (design smart transportation systems for cities).

Jim asked Wayne to post an oversized Valuable Work Detector on the office wall and write in at least one element related to FLR's latest strategy decision. Wayne quickly matched his personal Value Proposition with three PINT elements.

Jim smiled with satisfaction as he watched Wayne lay out a potent new way he could contribute to FLR. *These tools sure have made my job easier, he thought. Focusing on an external object and a physical task makes all the difference.* The HR director shook his head as he thought of the years he had spent working in a very different way.

Within the hour both men saw with startling clarity that Wayne was ideally positioned to head up the new smart transportation systems initiative within FLR. Days later the CEO agreed to the move. Now, Wayne was happily on his way to bigger things at FLR—and Jim enjoyed the warm afterglow of true leadership.

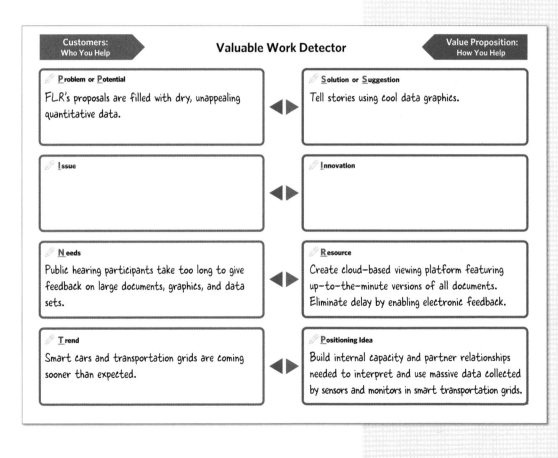

Valuable Work Detector

Customers: Who You Help

Value Proposition: How You Help

Problem or **P**otential
FLR's proposals are filled with dry, unappealing quantitative data.

Solution or **S**uggestion
Tell stories using cool data graphics.

Issue

Innovation

Needs
Public hearing participants take too long to give feedback on large documents, graphics, and data sets.

Resource
Create cloud-based viewing platform featuring up-to-the-minute versions of all documents. Eliminate delay by enabling electronic feedback.

Trend
Smart cars and transportation grids are coming sooner than expected.

Positioning Idea
Build internal capacity and partner relationships needed to interpret and use massive data collected by sensors and monitors in smart transportation grids.

When Fitting In Is a Matter of *Skyle*

Skill + Style

Sometimes an individual's problems within a team have more to do with style than substance. In part, this is because leaders tend to have a one-dimensional view of talent. They over-focus on skill while missing the power of the behavioral style by which results are delivered. This combination of skill + delivery style (*skyle*) goes beyond what people *can* do to encompass *how they do it*. Good *skyle* means being comfortable and friendly with other people and creating fit with role, leader, team, organization, and Customers. Poor *skyle* means being uncomfortable or aloof around others or creating friction that diminishes results.

You can help people fit in—and improve your leadership—by becoming sensitive to your colleagues' delivery style. The first step is to recognize that peoples' professional identity includes personal styles that vary in effectiveness. When someone shows good operating style, a leader's challenge is to support its continued use—and discourage overuse. A suboptimal style calls for early and possibly frequent coaching.

When someone exhibits poor style, broaching a conversation about change can be tough. If the skill level is adequate, though, and the real issue is style, you can balance the discussion by discussing both. A good way to do this is by using another third object tool: Skyle Zones.

Skyle Zones

Skyle Zones is a four-quadrant matrix showing skill level on the horizontal axis and style effectiveness on the vertical axis. For example, someone with low skill and an ineffective style scores in the lower left quadrant: The Oh, No! Zone. Someone with strong skills and good style scores in the upper right quadrant: The Flow Zone, and so forth.

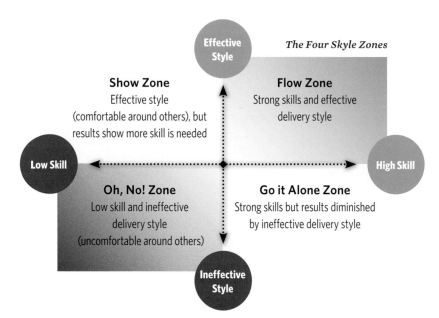

The Four Skyle Zones

Effective Style

Show Zone
Effective style (comfortable around others), but results show more skill is needed

Flow Zone
Strong skills and effective delivery style

Low Skill

High Skill

Oh, No! Zone
Low skill and ineffective delivery style (uncomfortable around others)

Go it Alone Zone
Strong skills but results diminished by ineffective delivery style

Ineffective Style

Remember Randy, the advertising account manager? His boss, Ellen, reviewed Skyle Zones with him, and described how Randy had wound up in the Go it Alone Zone during his last client presentation. Racing through one creative strategy after another, Randy failed to notice that the client wanted to ask for hard data following the presentation of each option. In short, he was more focused on his own ideas than the client's interests.

After reminding Randy of his strengths as both "entertainer" and "professor," Ellen described several missed client cues that he could have used to shift styles from "entertainer" to "professor" during the meeting. They agreed on some signals she would give him in future meetings if she sensed the need for a shift. With that, Randy was equipped to adapt his style to better support his team—and experience greater personal success.

Skyle Zones gives leaders and those they lead a way to focus discussions on performance and specify needed adjustments. Before using Skyle Zones with someone, make sure to prepare specific observations and behavioral descriptions of how others have reacted to that person. This may require gathering feedback from peers or other colleagues. Avoid relying solely on your own opinion or reactions.

All leaders risk hiring skilled people who turn out to be unable (or unwilling) to fulfill a team or organization's needs due to their ineffective style. Too often, leaders or hiring managers mistakenly assume that "skills" will create and sustain success, only to discover that the style of delivering those skills undermines it.

Now, get some experience with Skyle Zones by trying the exercise on the next pages.

Things to Try
on Monday Morning

Help Someone Improve Their Skyle

Skyle Zones can help you through difficult conversations with people. Try it with someone who needs to push a positive style toward the Flow Zone, or adapt an ineffective style that is keeping them in the Oh, No! or Go it Alone zones. Skyle Zones keeps the conversation objective, focusing it on behavior rather than personality.

Session 1. Ask a team member or direct report to have a conversation about the skills and styles they use in their work. Explain Skyle Zones and how it keeps conversations about work style objective and constructive. As homework, ask them to make a Skyle Zones sheet, jot down on sticky notes several behaviors they have recently shown, then place each note in the appropriate zone. Tell them you will do the same, and at the next session you will compare notes.

Session 2. When you meet again, seek first to understand—then to be understood. Carefully examine their Skyle Zones sheet. Ask about their behavior descriptions until you understand (not necessarily agree with) the behaviors identified. If the person accurately identified a problematic or desirable behavior, agree with their assessment and discuss next steps. Be sure to acknowledge and pay attention to behaviors they identified—but that you missed or with whose placement on the sheet you disagree. This is valuable feedback and may produce the insight needed for improvement.

The behavior you want to discuss may only be noted on your Skyle Zones sheet. If so, point this out. Be sure to describe the behavior with 1) objective observations (preferably from multiple sources), and 2) ensuing results (or lack of results). Discuss, then agree on what the preferred style should look like.

If you found it difficult to identify specific behaviors for this particular person, imagine how much harder it will be with people with whom you spend even less time! Yet those colleagues need your feedback, too. Consider making a habit of recording *skyle*-related observations.

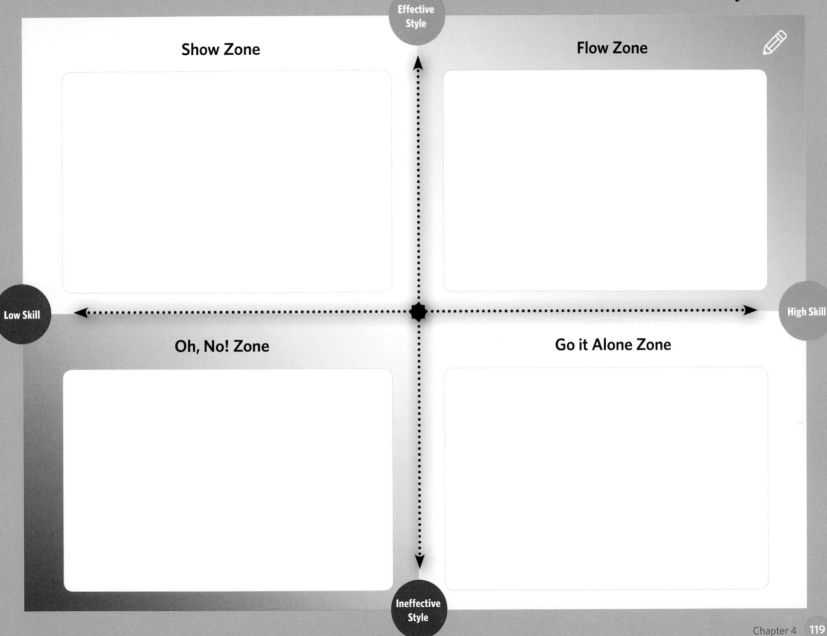

Show Zone

Flow Zone

Oh, No! Zone

Go it Alone Zone

Effective Style

Ineffective Style

Low Skill

High Skill

A Quick Review—and What's Next

A Quick Review

A personal business model drawn with a Canvas clarifies the logic by which an individual delivers value to Customers and is rewarded with both "hard" and "soft" benefits. Most important, it sets a personal Value Proposition that can be compared with team or enterprise Value Propositions.

Professional identity describes a person's occupational essence: specific results delivered, together with the style by which they are delivered.

The personal style by which value is delivered is a critical element of professional identity. Successful delivery requires a combination of skill and style (*skyle*). Use Skyle Zones to evaluate and give feedback when colleagues need to adjust their styles to better serve teams and achieve more personal success.

What's Next?

What should you do, though, when a competent worker fails to contribute to your team's goal? Or when someone you supervise turns out to be less than competent? How can you pursue team goals while serving as an effective mentor at the same time? Chapter 5 extends the Bigger Theory of Work to address these challenges—and offers new ways to solve them.

Section III

Teamwork

Boost teamwork with new tools that complement business model thinking.

Chapter 5

Begin With *Me*

Begin With *Me*

For leaders, few things are more rewarding than seeing someone thrive thanks to your guidance and encouragement. And few things are more difficult than disciplining, reassigning, or terminating workers. No single leadership strategy can both ease the difficulties and assure the rewards. But most leaders agree that—were it possible—the ability to directly touch what motivates people would be extraordinarily valuable.

Intrinsic Motivator	Definition
Purpose	The yearning to do what we do in the service of something larger than ourselves
Autonomy	The desire to direct our own lives
Relatedness	The urge to be recognized by and connected to others
Mastery	The drive to improve our skill at doing something that matters

What motivates people in the workplace is now a matter of scientific fact. Research conducted over decades has identified four intrinsic human motivators: *Purpose, Autonomy, Relatedness,* and *Mastery*.[1] Each of these four motivators is described in the table at left. See if you agree that they hold true for you, too.

The question for leaders, then, is not what motivates people—it is how to tap into the four motivators. What comes closest to putting your hands directly on the levers of behavior?

The answer is simple. But understanding it requires some background logic.

First, it is clear that leaders must somehow link team or enterprise goals to intrinsic motivators at the individual level. As people develop, at no point will you see them express an inherent desire to increase fourth quarter earnings or introduce the next software upgrade by next summer or double the number of successful adoptions at a social service agency. Such goals are organizational milestones that motivate leaders of traditional organizations. But what motivates individuals is *Purpose, Autonomy, Relatedness,* and *Mastery*.

That means the most common approach to motivation—mechanically promoting alignment with team or organizational goals without addressing very human motivations—will end up disappointing both parties. Leaders need a way to simultaneously address all four human motivators. Consider each of the four and how it relates to work:

Purpose: Work means helping other people. Individuals can understand who their organization helps by learning the enterprise business model. They can also find purpose in helping others do their jobs better.

Autonomy: People can learn to manage their own work lives, especially with guidance from a good leader. "Autonomy" is used here in the psychological sense of *agency* or *self-efficacy*, not independence from a group. Few people like being told what to do; most enjoy being part of a team.

Relatedness: For many people, the workplace provides a strong sense of belonging and social interaction. And recognition by a formal authority figure is a powerful motivator for almost everyone.

Mastery: The workplace is where most people build skills and experience. Leaders who facilitate this earn loyalty and respect.

These four motivators are also provided by family, friends, hobbies, sports, faith, and other pursuits. But for most people, the workplace—and work itself—is the key source of the four motivators. And for most people, various forms of work gel over time into what is called *career*. Career is a single concern that directly touches all four intrinsic motivators—the levers that trigger behavior. And the current state of anyone's career can be concisely expressed in the form of a single-sheet Personal Business Model. If you are wondering how to motivate people, knock on the door marked **career**.

Career Collaboration

The nice thing about careers is that everybody has one! And while some people move through theirs more elegantly than others, most are keen to go as far as possible as quickly as possible. Good leaders recognize this concern, and engage others by helping them in a way few leaders do: they show them how to progress *by doing the work of the team or enterprise*. Career collaboration is a powerful way for leaders to tap into individual motivation.

Career collaboration means helping someone manage their relationship to work by acting on intrapersonal, interpersonal, and market-based insights.[2]

Here is an uncomfortable truth: most people take on a more-or-less haphazard **series of jobs** that, over time, hopefully coalesces around a general theme. In short, most careers develop by default rather than by design. This hands-off approach to professional progress is called "spending your career getting one-job-in-a-row."[3] Most people would prefer to rise above the one-job-in-a-row approach and become truly engaged with their work. To do this, they need a Bigger Theory of Work—one that links their workplace behavior to both team goals and personal progress.

Career collaboration offers both a Bigger Theory of Work and the tools to put that theory into practice. Career collaboration puts primary responsibility for development squarely on the individual. But the leader regularly provides feedback and guidance to help the person develop by accomplishing the work of the team—and the enterprise.

How to Unify Different Generations in the Workplace

To attract and retain talented people, organizations have spent much effort parsing worker cohorts—Baby Boomers, Millennials, Generation Z 'screenagers,' and so forth—and struggled to figure out how they should address the differences between these cohorts. But rather than worrying about cohort differences, why not focus on what unites the generations? Every generation shares a crucial overarching element—an element common to every worker at every level in every enterprise: **career.**

Unseen Evidence, in Plain Sight

The U.S.-based Gallup Corporation is a research and performance-management consulting firm that has amassed data on 25 million employees worldwide. The company uses a simple, 12-question survey dubbed Q12 to assess engagement, which it defines as *workers' emotional commitment to their leaders*. Examining Gallup's Q12 shows that nearly half the questions are directly related to career concerns:

Q12 Engagement Question	Lesson for Leaders
1. At work I have the opportunity to do what I do best every day	Career progress lies in developing expertise and mastery, not achieving promotions
2. My supervisor or someone at work seems to care about me as a person	A personal relationship with a leader is essential for people to feel *valued*, not merely *evaluated*
3. There is someone at work who encourages my development	People want leaders to help them progress at work
4. In the last six months someone at work has talked to me about my progress	Growth requires regular feedback from a leader
5. This last year, I have had opportunities at work to learn and grow	Good leaders value individual *development*, not just individual *productivity*

Separate research shows that the most common reason for leaving an organization is lack of opportunity for progress.[4] Other research found that most employers believe leaders and colleagues should jointly "own" the career management process.[5]

Here is the irony: Most of the engagement improvement programs offered by consulting firms focus on recruiting, benefits and rewards programs, leadership training, better communications, and more frequent surveys. To be sure, none of these activities *reduce* employee engagement. But they funnel already-scarce leadership resources toward matters that fail to satisfy the crucial need for career collaboration. Today, few leaders teach people how to keep moving forward. What will you teach yours?

Career Collaboration Framework: The Three Questions

Three critical questions—whether consciously voiced or not—underpin the decisions of people who are striving to make progress at work. The Three Questions address the entire universe of possibilities for career-related action. As you read this section, adopt the viewpoint of yourself as a career-seeking professional.

1Q

Is it time to Move Up?

When you like your profession, your organization, and your role—and you want to progress—it may be time to *Move Up. Moving Up means progressing, not necessarily getting a promotion.* People define progress differently. For some, it may mean greater responsibility and higher compensation. For others, it may mean shifting into a more satisfying role, regardless of rank or compensation.

2Q

Is it time to Move Out?

When there is no longer a good fit with your profession, organization, or role, it may be time to *Move Out.* Note that "moving out" can mean staying with the same organization but moving out of a team or role (or separating from a supervisory relationship) that is no longer a good fit. Forward-thinking leaders understand that discussing "moving out" options is not the same as questioning loyalty. True leaders want to find the best place for people to exercise their talent.

3Q

Is it time to Adapt Your Style?

When you like your profession, your organization, and your role—but are falling short of the progress you want—it may be time to *Adapt Your Style.* Note two things: First, stagnation is most likely your own responsibility rather than someone else's fault. Second, competence is probably not the issue. Instead, it is likely there is something about the style by which you deliver value that can be adapted to better fit your circumstances. Identifying and addressing a needed style change requires good feedback and coaching (see page 116 for a review of work delivery style).

Five Things to Remember About the Three Questions

First, everyone must answer the Three Questions over and over again. This is not because they give the wrong answers each time! It is because people constantly evolve as individuals, as do the markets in which they work. That means people must regularly modify their personal business models: Adapting Style, Moving Out to a different team or new boss, or Moving Up to contribute more effectively to a group's purpose.

Second, there is no need to ask the Three Questions daily. The questions come into play only for those who sense the need for professional change—or when external forces demand it.

Third, leaders who use the Three Questions demonstrate through action that they are serious about both their own and other people's development. Through their actions, they ask others to assume responsibility for undertaking work that supports team goals. This shared responsibility eases the burden on leaders who are already hard-pressed to devote more time to coaching.

Fourth, the Three Questions approach legitimizes both the leader's and the individual's need to openly discuss Move Up, Move Out, and Adapt Style options. People can contemplate their work and make choices in the privacy of their own minds. But it is far more effective for people to contemplate the Three Questions aloud with a leader and mutually agree how their talent can best be deployed within a team or enterprise. The approach turns professional development—often a passive intellectual concept—into a concrete activity.

Finally, using the Three Questions eases difficult work-related conversations.

How to Use the Three Questions

Many leaders dread discussing performance, professional progress, "fit," transfers, or terminations with people they supervise. These conversations can be tense, awkward, and fraught with emotion. That is where the Three Questions can help. They give the discussion partners a shared vocabulary and a neutral "handle" to comfortably grasp and describe three possibilities for career-altering decisions. When both parties understand the approach, an invitation to "have a Three Questions conversation" signals a constructive, candid discussion using an agreed-upon vocabulary. This defuses tension and makes tough conversations easier. Once you have become familiar with the method yourself, here is a proven five-step process you can try with colleagues:

1. Prepare

A Three Questions conversation requires that both parties prepare. Ask your partner(s) to study the questions. Lend them this book, or provide them with the free materials available online. Understanding the concept and the vocabulary beforehand is essential. Preparation is what allows these conversations to be both brief and effective.

2. Invite

Invite your colleague to "have a Three Questions conversation" in a few days or a week's time. Ask them to prepare two things for the meeting: 1) an "as-is" personal business model, and 2) their thoughts (not necessarily written out) on which one of the Three Questions seems most compelling at the moment. For your part, you should be prepared to discuss your team's "as-is" business model.

3. Engage

Here is one proven way to conduct this meeting:

a. Ask, "Which question seems most relevant to you at this time?"

b. After hearing the response, avoid immediately discussing the chosen question. Instead, *talk about the other two questions first*. For example, you might say, "Interesting—let's come back to that question in a moment. But first, tell me some thoughts and feelings that arise when you think about the other two questions." You could prompt your partner to imagine work scenarios that come to mind under either of the other two questions. Or you could ask your partner to use their personal business model Canvas to show what the other two questions might mean.

c. Return to the originally chosen question. Ask why that question seemed most compelling at the beginning of the discussion. Then, probe whether the question still seems most relevant in light of comments from b) above. Ask your partner to confirm which question now seems most compelling.

d. If you agree with your partner, together sketch out a new "to be" personal business model that responds to the agreed-upon question (or assign that task as homework for a later meeting). If you disagree with the choice of question, you might say, "Share reasons why you thought that question was most compelling." You can then offer:

- Comments on behavior or delivery style
- Observations on results achieved or missed
- Insights into team business models relevant to the person's development

If neither of you feels a compelling need or desire to change anything, the meeting is over. The point of these conversations is not to be compulsively changing or "fixing" things. Sometimes you just need to confirm that all is going well. Keep calm and carry on! If one or both of you feels a compelling need or desire for change, go to Step 4.

4. Exit

Close the meeting. Offer a day or three for your partner to think about the session and return with a revised personal model. If you work in a smaller organization, you may feel you cannot offer much in terms of formal advancement. But other options are usually available. As career collaborators, you and your partner might explore moving elsewhere in the organization, taking on a "stretch" assignment, cross-training with another colleague, trying JobCrafting,[6] or taking other action that facilitates growth without a formal promotion. The key is to prevent people from becoming passive—or feeling entitled to advancement. If someone unrealistically feels entitled to a promotion, it is best to hold an honest *Move Out* or *Adapt Style* discussion rather than simply to hope things will work out.

5. Follow-up

Conduct a second Three Questions conversation to review the colleague's revised personal model. Remember, this is a partnership, so you want to start by setting the tone of working on the "to be" model together. It is not an all or nothing presentation by your colleague. Review the most compelling of the Three Questions that is being addressed by your colleague's model. Review the insights and feedback they are considering in the design of their model. You are now in a coaching role and providing a reality check on the possibilities presented in the "to be" model. This is a good time to reiterate one of the key facts about modeling: it is iterative. You may only use and implement part of the "to be" model based on current circumstances and resources. That is a modeling success. Be sure to conclude with a clear understanding of what each party will do to implement the "to be" model. The primary responsibility stays with the employee, but you may need to take action or provide resources.

When starting out, it is important to conduct Three Questions discussions more frequently. Strive for a 20 minute session every four to six weeks. Later, you can scale back to once every three months or so. The point is to make Three Questions conversations frequent enough that you spot people taking action that responds to their biggest growth challenges or opportunities. As with all discussions, the sooner feedback follows behavior, the greater the impact. Just prior to or following completion of a big project, for example, is a good time for a Three Questions conversation.

1Q

Is it time to **Move Up?**

2Q

Is it time to **Move Out?**

3Q

Is it time to **Adapt Your Style?**

Handling the Toughest Conversation

Many managers prefer to avoid career-related discussions and just hope things work out. But hope is not a strategy. It is helpful for both leaders and those they supervise to understand why performance-related conversations are often awkward or even contentious: it is because leaders must simultaneously support both who they work for and who they work with.

Sometimes, what your group needs is something a team member cannot deliver. This is a bad situation for everyone. If your people have been carefully recruited and well-trained, this will be rare. But with certain people, legitimate mismatches will arise—and stay unresolved. That is when you may need to broach the toughest conversation: *Is it time to Move Out?*

First, remember that Moving Out does not necessarily mean leaving the organization. It can mean moving out of a particular role or relationship with a certain leader, or out of a relationship with a team and being redeployed where strengths and weaknesses are better harmonized with the work. The ultimate Move Out, of course, means leaving the organization altogether. This could be based on poor individual performance or on issues beyond the individual's control, such as an economic downturn or a service or product discontinuance.

Moving Out is often driven by poor fit, but most people initially experience it as failure. Leaders need to set the context with some basic ideas:

1. Professional progress requires more than talent—it requires the right context. If an individual is skilled but poorly equipped to get along with certain Customers or colleagues, it may be time to move out.

2. *All jobs are temporary.* All jobs evolve as Customers, markets, or the organization changes.

3. Moving Out discussions must be based on evidence. Evidence is not limited to productivity statistics. Leaders can speak frankly about excessive time required to accomplish work, distracting emotional responses produced by a certain delivery style, or need for excessive help to accomplish work.

Tough Love Boosts Employer Brand

Not every leader has the emotional intelligence or interpersonal skills needed to handle difficult discussions. A U.S. transportation engineering firm solved this problem by pairing two leaders with complementary skills to conduct a tough Move Out discussion with a talented but misplaced engineer. Months later, the two leaders were surprised when the terminated engineer visited to thank them for "helping me understand what 'better fit' means instead of letting me stay stuck in the wrong role." The episode transformed a terminated employee into a goodwill ambassador—and elevated the firm's brand as an employer.

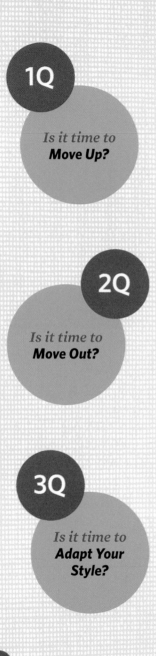

1Q

Is it time to
Move Up?

2Q

Is it time to
Move Out?

3Q

Is it time to
**Adapt Your
Style?**

A Three Questions Beginner's Mistake

Karen served as general manager for a diversified producer of foods, including frozen dough and ready-to-bake pastries that require highly specialized machinery. She faced a problem with Allen, a division manager who oversaw frozen food production. Allen was a brilliant production machinery technician, but the work teams he supervised were growing louder in their complaints about his angry, condescending workstyle. Karen frowned as she thought about her upcoming meeting with Allen. The situation called for more than a reprimand, but Karen wanted to keep things constructive. She had read about Three Questions and decided to give the approach a try.

At the meeting, Karen explained the Three Questions and asked which question Allen thought was most relevant. The conversation quickly collapsed, and ended with Karen issuing a flustered ultimatum: *Adapt your style or move out!*

Afterward, Karen realized the situation involved personality issues beyond her expertise, so she asked the human resources director to find a coach for Allen. At their first session, the coach quickly discovered that, while Allen loved nothing better than to solve baffling technical problems, he failed to recognize his own problem-solving gifts. As a result, he assumed others should foresee and prevent problems the way he did. This led to his angry, condescending style of troubleshooting problems in real time in front of humiliated work crews. The coach confirmed Allen's abrasive style through brief private interviews with several coworkers.

At their second meeting, the coach asked Allen, "Is this management role something you truly want? It does not seem to suit your style and temperament." Within the relaxed privacy of this conversation, Allen was able to admit the truth. "I love troubleshooting, but I really don't like managing people."

The solution? Allen stayed with the company but moved out of his management role. Expert engineering troubleshooting was needed in many areas, so Karen and Allen agreed to recast Allen as an internal consultant. Allen retained his title but was relieved of staff management responsibilities. The entire company benefited from this change.

Lessons Learned

Share the Methodology First

Karen tried to remedy a crisis by using the Three Questions, when the situation would have been better served by adopting the method *before* problems arose. At the least, she might have asked Allen to study the Three Questions approach beforehand and prepare himself for "a Three Questions conversation." Instead, she made a classic teaching mistake: teaching a new skill while simultaneously forcing its application in high-pressure circumstances.

Recognize the Importance of *Skyle*

Karen correctly sensed the importance of personality in this situation. But she could have done better by recognizing earlier that colleagues deliver their value not through skill alone, but through a combination of skill and *style*, or *skyle*. Sensitivity to the importance of *skyle* might have eliminated the need for a third-party coach. Many professional development conversations derail when the employee legitimately claims that their skill level is adequate to the task. Meanwhile, the leader is trying to focus on the *style* by which that skill is delivered. It pays to teach people the difference between skill and style—and what *skyle* means to their professional progress.

Trust is Key

Karen's authority intimidated Allen and kept him from trusting her enough to disclose a difficult-to-admit truth. But revealing that truth, it turns out, helped Allen *progress professionally*. The Three Questions build mutual trust by explicitly recognizing that career collaboration is a joint effort to help talented people achieved greater success—and address problems before they harm an entire team.

Helping *Me* Progress

Leaders who practice the Three Questions agree to help people regularly reality-check their professional progress within the organization and examine *Move Up*, *Move Out*, and *Adapt Style* options. In return, those colleagues agree to "own" their professional growth and to be responsible for 1) understanding the relevant team or enterprise business model under which they operate, and 2) understanding their own personal business model and how it contributes to the higher model(s).

Both team and personal business models evolve over time. Personal models often move in step with life changes: getting married, having children, undergoing illness or divorce, gaining spiritual awareness, growing older, caring for aging parents, or any of a hundred other experiences.

Team business models, meanwhile, may evolve even more quickly. All enterprise (and thus team) models eventually become outmoded. But until they do, they change due to new strategic priorities, reorganizations or acquisitions, new leadership, or shifts in the technological, economic, social, or competitive environment. As a consequence, leadership success has much to do with the ability to move back and forth between dealing with personal and team business models—and to give guidance that keeps the two aligned. This task demands insight and sensitivity to how personal and team models change over time.

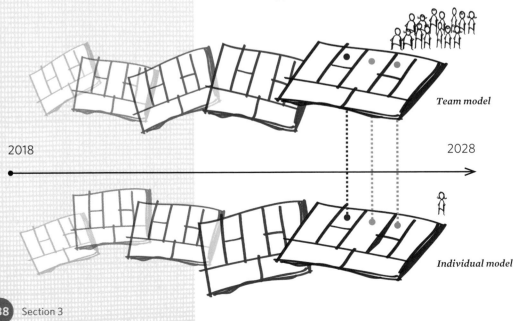

2018

2028

Team model

Individual model

A New View of Career Development

Career development was traditionally viewed as a series of *choices*. Three Questions views careers as a series of *changes*. The traditional view also presumed advancement in step with chronological age. But rapid social change and technological innovation have rendered age considerations obsolete. Consider some workers whom you might find yourself helping:

- A 45-year-old mother who, after 17 years of parenting, returned to school to earn an MBA in healthcare management. In the classroom, she sat next to 26-year-olds who later competed with her for junior management roles in the post-graduation marketplace. Traditional career development models would not have predicted this scenario.

- A 22-year-old robotics enthusiast with six years of formal and informal experience is working on smartphone location apps. She beat out 35-year-old rivals for a senior development position in a startup focused on global positioning systems.

- A 50-year-old lawyer and father of two, unable to ignore his passion for flying and sailing, entered an aeronautical engineering program where he competed with 23-year-old math whizzes. Yet his first post-graduate job at the Jet Propulsion Laboratory demanded his judgment skills as much as his engineering expertise.

Today it is more useful for leaders to think of career as unattached to age (and less attached to formal experience), and to focus on accelerating worker progress at any age. What follows is a model that will help you do just that.

The Five-Stage Career Model

The Five-Stage Career Model says that, throughout their working lives, people pass through one or more of five stages. These stages are not defined by seniority, role longevity, or chronological age. Rather, they are defined by the desire to progress. Answering The Three Questions help people decide whether they should move to the next stage, remain in the current stage, or even return to a previous stage.

The Five-Stage model is value-neutral; it defines no "correct" or "desirable" path. Some people (maybe even most people) reach only Stage Two, for example. Others travel through several stages, then return to a previous stage. Still others experience all five—then start over! Again, the Five-Stage model proscribes no right or wrong path. Rather, it establishes a shared vocabulary so everyone can discuss professional progress constructively and with a minimum of unproductive tension. The five stages are:

Stage 1. Test Your Training
Stage 2. Develop Your Specialty
Stage 3. Lead Your Specialty
Stage 4. Lead More Complexity or Beyond Your Specialty
Stage 5. Lead Even Greater Complexity or Start Over

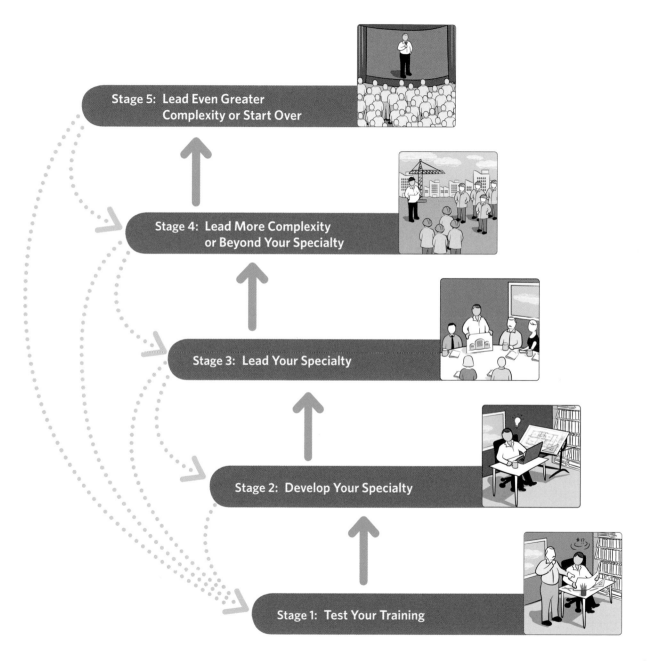

Stage 5: Lead Even Greater Complexity or Start Over

Stage 4: Lead More Complexity or Beyond Your Specialty

Stage 3: Lead Your Specialty

Stage 2: Develop Your Specialty

Stage 1: Test Your Training

Stage 1. Test Your Training

Imagine you are supervising a new high-school, trade-school, or college graduate starting her first serious, full-time job. She needs to "test her training"—to discover if she likes the work, whether it meets her expectations, if her training or preparation was adequate, and what the future might hold. The table on the facing page shows questions she is likely to ask herself—and things you can say to facilitate her progress. This stage is closely related to the *Who You Are* and *What You Do* (Key Resources and Key Activities) building blocks of the personal business model, because it involves testing knowledge and initial ability to achieve results.

Keep in mind that Stage 1 is also experienced by people like Joan, a 41-year-old history teacher who left education to attend law school, and is now starting to practice law for the first time. Or by Thomas, a 30-year-old machinist who worked for a metal fabricator, but after earning a mechanical engineering degree sought greater technical challenge by joining a local aerospace parts manufacturer, where he is now testing his training.

Stage 1. Questions for Colleagues and Their Leaders

What people in Stage 1 often ask themselves:	What you can say to accelerate progress:
Does this work really fit me?	"Tell me about the aspects of this work that you find most comfortable and satisfying. Contrast that with the aspects that you find difficult or unsatisfying."
Have I been naïve about this occupation?	"What has surprised you most about this role and the work you have been doing?"
Did my training adequately prepare me for the real work in this industry?	"If you could go back and pursue more or different training or education to prepare for this work, what would you do differently?"
Do I like the work? My colleagues? My organization?	"Describe what I would see if I watched you in your *current role* at your best and at your emotional highest. Who is there? What is happening? What is your purpose? Be specific in describing this scenario."
What would be a good niche for me to develop?	"Describe what I would see if I watched you in *an ideal next role* at your best and at your emotional highest. Who is there? What is happening? What is your purpose? Be specific in describing this scenario."
How can I adapt my approach to the work so that I earn even more responsibility and access to more significant work?	"I would like you to learn how others perceive your *skyle* by using tools such as: - a 360 feedback instrument - Having a human resources person interview a few of your colleagues or customers - Directly soliciting colleague feedback via e-mail, phone, or face-to-face talks - Taking a proficiency test that measures ability to do certain work"

Stage 2. Develop Your Specialty

Stage 1 gives people the opportunity to understand what they do best and enjoy most: a chance to claim occupational ground upon which they can build their Professional Identity. People who successfully test their training and find a good fit within Stage 1 will naturally seek to advance to Stage 2. Stage 2 is where people develop a specialty and a reputation within a specific domain. Stage 2 is closely related to the *How You Help* (Value Proposition) building block of the personal business model, because people must build their reputations for producing results. Reputation for results starts to matter more than deeper content knowledge (further education) or technical skill (more training) characteristic of Stage 1.

For example, during Stage 1, Thomas, the machinist, demonstrated outstanding precision and care. So in Stage 2 he was entrusted to work on jet engine parts, for which extreme accuracy is crucial. He also demonstrated an ability to rapidly understand other skilled colleagues' work and developed relationships easily around the design shop.

During Stage 1, Joan, the history teacher–turned lawyer, quickly discovered that corporate law was a poor fit. Thanks to an astute leader, she relocated within the firm to focus on family law. Then, in Stage 2, she developed a new specialty in child custody mediation, which effectively drew on her long experience working with adolescents and their parents.

Many people reach Stage 2 and comfortably spend the rest of their working lives there. Think of a mail carrier who is comforted by routine and loves working outdoors with minimal supervision. Combining those satisfying elements in another job would be difficult. Similarly, consider a high school history teacher who loves the subject, thrills to effecting change in student attitudes each year, and relishes serving as coach for the school's award-winning debate club. He might happily retire after 25 years as a classroom teacher.

If your organization values people staying at Stage 2 over the long term, you may need to provide specific rewards for doing so. Otherwise, people who perform best in Stage 2 may be tempted to pursue leadership roles they do not actually want, because it is the only way to obtain greater rewards.

Stage 2. Questions for Colleagues and Their Leaders

What people in Stage 2 often ask themselves:	What you can say to accelerate progress:
Has my education and experience fulfilled my expectations for finding satisfying work to the extent that I should stay in this niche?	"How has your training and education been tested at work to date? How would others describe the work that you are especially good at doing? How do you describe your specialty?"
If I stay and progress in my mastery of this work, what would the next level of specialty look like? Does the prospect of doing that work excite me?	"Are there special projects that you can see yourself working on? What kinds of work would stretch you a bit?"
Am I sought after for advice or my perspective on increasingly complex problems?	"Describe a time when you were identified and sought out as the 'go-to' person for a certain skill or insight."
Am I ready to lead others who do this work?	"Please try this Professional Identity exercise (page 110). The results can help you identify your leadership qualities."
Is it time to move up to a leadership role?	"Describe someone you know who has had a desirable career progression without becoming a manager or leader in their field."
Could managing/leading be as interesting as performing my specialty function?	"On your 'to-be' personal business model Canvas, show me some Key Activities that involve helping other people. How about a Value Proposition that benefits your colleagues?"

Stage 3. Lead Your Specialty

People who develop a good reputation are often asked to move into Stage 3 and assume management roles. The transition to Stage 3 is perhaps the most challenging of all, because a person's perspective and role must shift from self-management to managing others.

Stage 3 calls for new leaders to refocus on helping others become more effective. In particular, a new manager's capacity to notice individual Key Resources and Value Propositions and match them to the right work will be crucial to Stage 3 success.

Those who show talent for directing day-to-day work in Stage 3 may be given larger teams or more ambitious goals. This may mean transcending management and assuming a true *leadership* role: looking beyond day-to-day activities to envision and pursue a preferred future; developing policy rather than simply administering it; and recruiting and training people. It is helpful to distinguish between *formal* leadership (contractual authority over other workers) and *thought* leadership (informal or implied authority based on competence and reputation).

For example, Sushma, a chemist working in a medical school research laboratory, is both a thought leader and a formal leader. As a formal leader, she oversees both research work and the staff that runs the laboratory. She supervises other chemists and laboratory technicians, but she does not run experiments or operate equipment herself. As a thought leader, though, she designs the research that will advance her team's understanding of cancer cells.

Sophia, on the other hand, is a manufacturing specialist who arranges on-site training at newly-constructed fabrication facilities. Her promotion to Stage 3 required directly supervising trainers, so she assumed formal management authority. Over time she may move into a true leadership role.

Finally, consider Joan, the attorney. Three years after being hired, she was invited to join the firm's management committee. She accepted the challenge, and is now managing other adult professionals: a role for which she never formally trained or prepared. As she learns her new role, she may feel a bit disjointed or "not herself." In this smaller law firm, she will be responsible for both tactical management and planning future strategy, meaning she will have a combined management/leadership role. Only time will tell if this new role suits her more than practicing her family law specialty.

Stage 3. Questions for Colleagues and Their Leaders

What people in Stage 3 often ask themselves:	What you can say to accelerate progress:
Is managing/leading as interesting as performing my specialty function?	"What have you liked most and least about leading? Do you miss anything about your previous role?"
How do I feel about focusing more on other people's productivity than on my own?	"Can you describe specific ways people became more productive due to your leadership? How would you describe the difference between coaching vs. managing someone?"
Am I headed toward a new career called 'management'?	"Describe an area of expertise where you are doing less work than before. Who does that work now instead of you?"
How can I gain enough influence to correct processes that need adjusting?	"Communicating persuasively is crucial for managers. Do you have a model for improving your persuasion skills? If not, you might try *Harnessing the Science of Persuasion* by Robert Cialdini or *The Necessary Art of Persuasion* by Jay Conger." "Here is an Alignment Canvas. Show me how your group aligns with the higher model."
Is it time to move up to a more complex leadership role?	"Outside of your current specialty, which groups do you interact with most? With which groups do you have the most influence?"

Some new managers discover that their strengths or satisfactions remain at Stage 2 (Develop Specialty). For example, Sophia, the manufacturing expert, became a training manager but fared poorly. She paid too much attention to the details of how her trainers presented their courses (her old Stage 2 job) and failed to develop her new management role. She might have enjoyed success if a perceptive leader had used Three Questions to coach her to adapt her style away from micromanaging and toward finding new internal Customers for her training team to serve.

Stage 4. Lead More Complexity or Beyond Your Specialty

The experience of leading a specialty in Stage 3 takes people to a career crossroads. Those who were successful and enjoyed Stage 3 may find themselves keen to advance to Stage 4: *leading more complexity within the specialty or leading beyond the specialty.* On the other hand, those who enjoyed less success or "fit" may wish to remain in Stage 3—or even return to Stage 2 and refocus on developing their own specialties, unburdened by management responsibility.

Very few people reach Stage 4. Doing so requires a comprehensive understanding of the enterprise model and the relationships between lower models. Technical skills becomes less important, because Stage 4 is about paying attention to the *interfaces* between specialized teams: teams that, while collaborating under their respective leaders' guidance, may simultaneously "compete" for attention and resources. People in Stage 4 will want to teach business models to clarify and coordinate the greater complexity they are expected to lead.

Lauren, for example, worked in an equipment division of telecommunications giant Motorola. This was an "up or out" team where, amid the organization's struggle to match the blistering pace of market change, workers who failed to learn and adapt were seen as bogging down more ambitious colleagues. *Moving Up* meant formal promotion to a higher title and salary and being asked to manage an additional function. Lauren moved up by agreeing to take over the marketing director's management duties while continuing to fulfill her sales leadership role. She was given a new title—Vice President of Sales and Marketing—a traditional promotion into multiple-function leadership.

One caution about adapting to a management or leadership role: during Stage 3 or Stage 4, it often becomes obvious when someone has been promoted beyond their level of competence (the so-called Peter Principle). In Stage 3, leadership is often a completely new role on top of the specialty the new leader worked years to perfect. Many new leaders find it comforting to return to being a specialist until they can better fulfill a leadership role. In Stage 4, some leaders discover that love of or loyalty to their professional specialty is too strong, and that paying attention to other areas is distracting or disheartening. Such leaders will do well to return to a previous stage.

Stage 4. Questions for Colleagues and Their Leaders

What people in Stage 4 often ask themselves:	What you can say to accelerate progress:
Am I losing touch with the 'art and science' of the work I used to love?	"How do you feel when you are with a new group of colleagues whose work is less familiar to you? What would you need to feel more comfortable with their problems, issues, needs, and trends?"
Is this more administrative work than I can tolerate?	"Where do you have the most difficulty prioritizing work, especially in the area that is new to you?"
How do I influence leaders in functional areas outside of my area (such as human resources)?	"Communicating persuasively is crucial for managers. Do you have a model for improving your persuasion skills? If not, you might try *Harnessing the Science of Persuasion* by Robert Cialdini or *The Necessary Art of Persuasion* by Jay Conger." "Here is an Alignment Canvas. Show me how your group aligns with the higher model."
How can I learn more about our competition?	"Use an enterprise Canvas to model a competitor. How do they operate differently from us? How might we emulate a portion of their model to improve what we do?"
How can I help refocus the company at a strategic level rather than just implementing best practices in my functional areas of responsibility?	"Use an Alignment Canvas to show an opportunity to modify a team model or the enterprise model."

Stage 5. Manage Even Greater Complexity or Start Over

For the rare person who finds success and satisfaction in all four previous stages, Stage 5 offers two ultimate challenges: 1) managing even greater complexity, or 2) starting over in a new role.

James provides an example of leading even greater complexity. He started out in Stage 1 as a human resources specialist with chipmaker Advanced Micro Devices (AMD), conducting studies of employee wellness programs with the goal of identifying the kinds of participation that actually reduced AMD's health and safety costs. His strong interest in how motivation impacts organizations eventually led him to testing instrument giant Tektronics, where he served in the ultimate Stage 3 role: as Vice President of Human Resources.

But James was destined to progress through all five stages. He moved out of HR to run a vertically integrated Tektronics unit that made fiber optic cable testing instruments, and in so doing became a Stage 4 leader of design, manufacturing, quality, marketing, and sales functions. Following success at this level, he was given the opportunity to move to Stage 5 and the highest level of complexity: president of a Tektronics subsidiary.

Tom, on the other hand, began Stage 1 at Intel as a junior production engineer. Over 28 years, he achieved his lifelong goal of managing an entire fabrication plant (Stage 5). Once he overcame the surprise of having accomplished this lifelong goal at the age of 50, he decided to start over at Stage 1 in a new "strategic human resources" role supporting product and service unit managers. Though he was new to human resources, his deep experience in CPU fabrication enabled him to serve as a mentor to upcoming leaders struggling with manufacturing and management challenges. Tom discovered that starting in a new role means once again paying attention to the personal business model elements of *What You Have* (Key Resource knowledge needed for the new role) and *What You Do* (Key Activity methods and processes needed to produce results).

Tom and James represent two different but very satisfying progressions to Stage 5. James moved up to the highest possible role within an organization. Tom moved out of his technical leadership role and rebooted his career in a new functional area: human resources. Stage 5 is about combining successes and competencies in a bold move of self-expression and ultimate professional development.

Stage 5. Questions for Colleagues and Leaders

What people in Stage 5 often ask themselves	What leaders can say to accelerate progress
Is it time to retire? Is it time to reinvent myself in an entirely new position?	"Draw a 'to-be' personal business model showing the next phase of your career."
Who are the future leaders of this organization, and how can I mentor or help them?	"Looking at your personal business model, how could you transfer Key Resources, Key Activities and Customer Relationships to colleagues? Who comes to mind when you think about potential transferees?"
Where would I like to be placed on the succession plan for this organization?	"Who do you know who has stayed with us in a traditional role? Who do you know who has stayed in a non-traditional role?"

Very few people progress through all five stages, and fewer still cycle through them more than once. Yet most people have family elders who experienced a traditional, lifelong progression through two or more of the Five Stages, all within a single organization, such as a metropolitan school district, a government body, or a corporate powerhouse such as Siemens, McKinsey & Company, or Toyota. And most people know someone who started over during one of the Five Stages and returned to a previous stage—even back to Stage 1. For example, the 45-year-old homemaker-turned healthcare MBA candidate will have to "test her training" after she exits the program with plenty of knowledge—but limited contemporary experience.

As a leader, think of the Three Questions as an internal gyroscope operating within each stage of a person's career, helping orient them toward greater professional progress. As those around you advance, you need to help them ask and answer the Three Questions *more than once*. Meanwhile, the Three Questions will keep you aware and conscious of your own career stage—and enable you to anticipate and determine optimal next steps. Start by trying the Three Questions exercise on the next page.

Things to Try
on Monday Morning

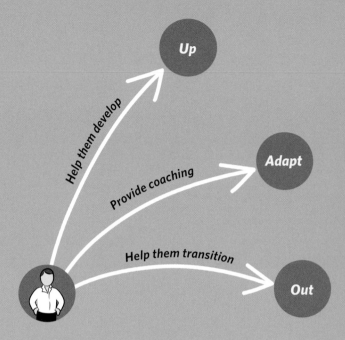

Three Questions Practice

This Three Questions exercise will help you accelerate teammate progress in the best direction: either Moving Up, Moving Out, or Adapting Style. As a leader, consider that Moving Up suggests development needs, Moving Out suggests transition needs, and Adapting Style suggests coaching needs.

Step 1

In the "Colleagues" row of the table below write the names of one, two, or three people you lead. Choose people you think might benefit from a Three Questions conversation: for example, one or more of your highest- or lowest-performing team members.

Step 2

Under each person's name, choose either the **Move Up? Move Out?** or **Adapt Style?** cell and briefly describe evidence suggesting why you think that Question is most relevant to the person at this time.

✎ Colleagues	1:	2:	3:
Move Up? Evidence of need to Move Up			
Move Out? Evidence of need to Move Out			
Adapt Style? Evidence of need to Adapt Style			

Step 3 ✎ Decide which colleague is most important for you to speak with first. Below, write what you will say when inviting them to have a Three Questions conversation:

Finally, which of the Three Questions is most relevant for *you* at this time? Do you have a colleague, friend, boss, or partner who could tell you which question they think is most relevant for you, and why? Ask.

Next Steps

Now that you have completed this chapter, you can look a teammate in the eye and say, in all sincerity, "I want to help you progress in your career."

You have learned that career is one thing all workers have in common that directly activates each of the four intrinsic human motivators: **Purpose, Autonomy, Relatedness,** and **Mastery**. A career can be described on a single-sheet Personal Business Model Canvas, creating a simple overview that facilitates discussion, insight, and most important, action.

Next, you learned how to boost engagement through *career collaboration*: helping people manage their relationship to work by acting on intrapersonal, interpersonal, and market-based insights. This collaboration is done using the Three Questions, a technique that replaces tense, formal discussions with relaxed, action-focused conversations.

Finally, the Five-Stage Career model gives you a contemporary way to view how your colleagues (and you!) advance as professionals. When you imagine what career stages your colleagues are in—and whether they might need to *Move Up, Move Out,* or *Adapt Style*—you gain insight into their personal and professional lives, and set yourself apart as a true leader.

If an organization's purpose is to be fulfilled, the people fulfilling it must believe that "it starts with me." It is not everyone else's responsibility, nor something leaders alone can achieve. So *we* begins with *me:* with understanding and supporting the individuals who comprise the teams that, in turn, comprise the organization.

Now it is time to see how others use the tools to match individual action with team goals—to align *me* with *we*.

Align *Me* With *We*

So far you have learned to use business models to depict organizations, teams, and individuals. Now it is time to work on aligning models to reduce the guesswork and conflict that people experience as they strive to work effectively in organizations. The most basic alignment is between organizational and individual models. Consider the experience of one growing U.S. company that essentially reinvented itself by aligning *me* with *we*.

Bob Fariss

FITNESS CENTER

Abandoning *What*, Starting Over With *Why*

Fitness center franchise Fit For Life had always promoted *what* it offered: beautiful facilities and fantastic equipment—things few members could afford to own themselves. But the U.S. recession that began in 2008 nearly killed the business: customers quit in droves after deciding that gym membership was, after all, a luxury. The owner brought in a new partner to turn things around.

The franchise's new CEO, Perry Lunsford, recognized that remaining members were those committed to long-term training programs—they did not consider gym memberships discretionary. Based on that insight, Perry, a fan of Simon Sinek's Golden Circle,[1]

decided to reverse the traditional gym strategy. Instead of focusing on Fit For Life's *what*—facility and equipment—he would promote Fit for Life's *why*: fitness and good health. Perry and his team defined their *why* as "to change people's lives."

The revamped company achieved good results by presenting life-changing personal fitness, rather than facility access, as the key membership benefit. Yet Fit For Life still faced a stiff challenge. It had successfully redesigned its strategy, but now it needed employees to commit to the new *why*: to align each individual *me* with the collective *we*.

Fit for Life's Application of The Golden Circle

We believe all lives can be changed for the better and find purpose in our own lives making that happen

The way we change lives for the better is through purposeful exercise programs

We sell affordable, effective fitness programs in beautiful, friendly facilities

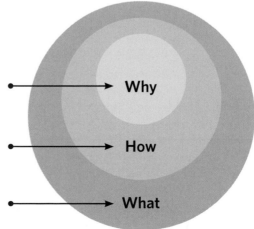

Why

How

What

Matching Personality and Activities, Sharing the *Why*

One big problem was that personal trainers served as the company's de facto training salesforce. Yet trainers are often weak salespeople, says Fit For Life CFO Bob Fariss. Bob used personal business models to analyze different roles within the company and gain insight into how the typical trainer's *skyle* was a poor match for selling.

"Your typical trainer is a wonderful, caring human being who really wants to help others and is therefore a bit uncomfortable asking for money," Bob says. "They often do not do well at closing sales, and because of that, many do not make enough money to survive in the job."

Hire People Who Believe What You Believe

Management realized it could no longer rely only on trainers to sell training. Instead, it needed to hire new people to sell both memberships and personal training services. At the same time, it needed to make sure all employees understood the new why—and were personally committed to changing people's lives. So Perry and his team crafted a new help-wanted advertisement—one that extended the company why to the personal level. Here is how Fit For Life's new ad read:

We do a lot of things really awesome. One of those things is sell personal training better than anyone else in the fitness industry. I was tired of watching great trainers go back to school to be firemen and nurses, because they couldn't feed their families when gyms didn't know how to feed them. Fit For Life has been in business since 1991 and over the years we have developed a sales process that changes people's lives. We change the lives of our franchisees, we change the lives of our members and most importantly for this post, we change the lives of our trainers! We give them the opportunity to make real money and to have a real career doing the thing they really love!

The first person hired from the new advertisement doubled his gym's sales conversion rate in his first four weeks. "The goal is not to hire people who need a job," says Bob. "As Simon Sinek says, the goal is to hire people who believe what you believe." Now, all Fit For Life staff get the *why*—here is a trainer's personal business model:

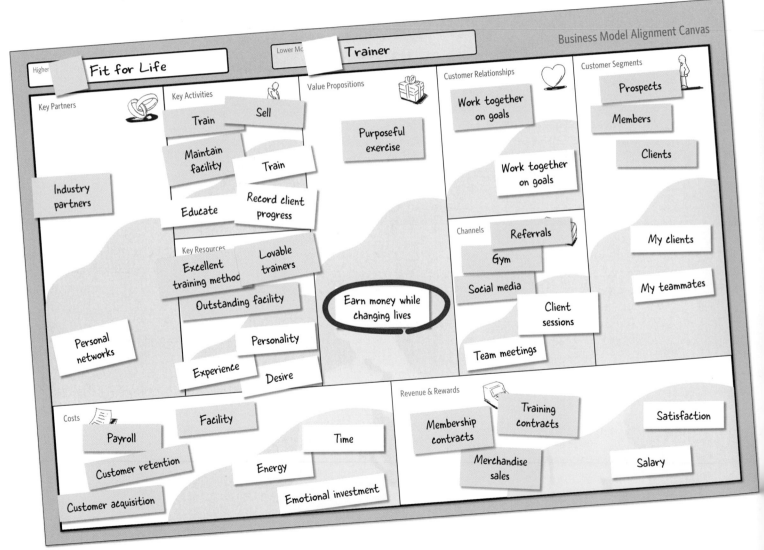

FITNESS CENTER

Extending the Power of Why

Commitment to the new *why* has grown beyond the salespeople. Perry, the CEO, now requires that all Fit For Life managers experience the *why* by taking personal training. "Everyone needs to personally experience our *why*," says Bob. "When I meet to discuss operational issues with our co-owner, Ken Stone—one of the most popular trainers in all of Texas—we start with a joint mixed martial arts training session. That gets our adrenaline going!"

The Fit For Life management team works hard to assure alignment between personal and group *whys*. But management does most of the business modeling. "People whose jobs involve a lot of physical activity and practical, manual work tend to be less interested in conceptual tools," says Bob.

But those employees respond well to graphics viewable online. So Bob created teamwork tables, then used a visualization tool to create infographics showing membership and training contract growth by location. He updates the infographics daily and shares them with team members via smart phone.

Now, Fit For Life teams enjoy competing with their colleagues at rival locations. A bonus: management views of the underlying data indicate when sales are a true team effort versus the results of a single charismatic performer.

"We started with *why,* used business modeling strategy, and now we improve tactics with third object team visualizations," says Bob. "However you go about it, you need to first align the *me* to the *we*."

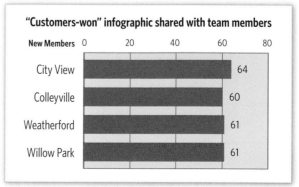

"Customers-won" infographic shared with team members

New Members	0	20	40	60	80
City View					64
Colleyville					60
Weatherford					61
Willow Park					61

Creating Connections:
Like Facebook on Paper

Fit For Life is convinced that aligning individual actions with group goals requires leaders to forge genuine personal connections with team members. That connection is crucial for recognizing and affirming each individual's worth—and assures that no worker suffers from anonymity. As Patrick Lencioni notes, all people need to be understood and appreciated for their unique qualities by someone in a position of authority.[2] Effective leaders understand that they must express genuine personal interest in the people who look to them for guidance. An ideal way for a leader to express that interest is by enabling personal business modeling in the workplace. Here is a complementary exercise that helps forge personal connections between people, whether they are already teammates or are meeting for the first time.

How it Was Used
The exercise was used for a subgroup of a large engineering and construction firm with more than 50,000 employees. Among other highly technical work, the subgroup members handled risk calculations related to managing hazardous waste. Most were men with masters or doctorate degrees in mathematics or engineering, 57 years old on average.

The group faced two challenges. First, the impending expiration of long-term facility management contracts was forcing the firm to become more entrepreneurial about seeking out and securing new work. Second, the young engineers and their older counterparts were not interacting, so younger engineers were failing to benefit from their col-

leagues' deep experience. Meanwhile, older engineers were missing exposure to the younger engineers' entrepreneurial drive.

Purpose
Facilitate mingling among older and younger engineers, build trust and rapport.

Method
Create a "Facebook on Paper"[3] mural that visually depicts participants and their common interests. Help people connect by discovering personal things they did not know about each other.

Number of Participants
In this instance: 28 people. The exercise can accommodate more if a large enough wall is available.

Time Needed
The initial exercise can be completed in 20 minutes or less. Anyone can return to the mural and add connections at any time.

Materials, Tools, other Requirements

1. Large, blank, contiguous wall
2. Paper measuring at least 1x5 meters (3x15 feet). Use a paper roll or tape together sheets of craft or butcher paper to create the mural
3. 7.5x12.5mm (3x5 inch) or larger cards or sticky notes for use as avatars, one per person
4. Pens or markers in multiple colors
5. Adhesive tape or other means for affixing avatars to mural

Instructions

1. Give an overview

"Today we're going to draw the social network that is in this room right now. We're going to make something like Facebook—on paper—using this wall!"

2. Create avatars using cards or notes

"First, we need the fundamental elements of the network: who you are. Create an avatar for yourself by writing on the card your name, short phrases describing your interests or experience—whatever you like. And if you like, draw a picture that represents you!" Share your own avatar amateur drawing, welcome laughs, and expect apologies for lack of drawing ability as participants create their avatars. Or bring an instant camera and have participants use photos of themselves on their avatars.

3. "Upload" avatars to the mural

Have everyone walk to the wall and "upload" their avatars anywhere they like. Demonstrate by uploading your own avatar first. Be sure plenty of adhesive tape is handy, especially if the group is large.

4. Draw connections

Finally, ask participants to identify connections by drawing lines between their avatars and avatars of people they know. Have them label these lines with identifiers such as "worked in software development" or "lived in Seattle." Then ask everyone to stroll along the mural and view the avatars of people they do not yet know, and encourage them to draw and label "connection" lines when they find something in common: "crazy about fishing," "dog lover," etc.

Result

The exercise produces a mural visually depicting newly discovered connections between members of an organization. The exercise is fun and builds a sense of community. The mural can remain on the wall and be added to by anyone at any time—consider appointing one person as "keeper of the mural" for the organization. In this case, a divisional human resources director participated and was thrilled with the intergenerational interactions created as younger and older engineers discovered common hobbies and personal interests.

Debriefing

Ask, *Did anyone make a surprising connection with someone they did not know before? Tell us about it.* In the situation described here, the facilitator could have said, *In this group, the mural represents shared interests and potential relationships that can be uncovered with a simple exercise. This is similar to the experience and market knowledge that can be uncovered and shared among long-standing and newer engineers in this group.* Facebook on Paper is mainly a relationship and trust-building exercise rather than one with a specific learning point, but debriefing remains important. Until you debrief, the exercise belongs to you rather than the participants.

Dennis Daems

A Comprehensive Approach to Aligning *Me* to *We* in the Enterprise

Here is a company that forges personal connections with potential employees *before* they are hired—then uses those connections to bring on the very best people available.

EIFFEL is a 500-person, Netherlands-based consultancy serving both for-profit and nonprofit clients in the insurance, healthcare, energy, and government sectors. EIFFEL clients have one thing in common: they face tough challenges making and executing strategic decisions in fast-moving markets, often amid close public scrutiny.

EIFFEL is distinctive in several ways. First, it boasts a strong heritage in sports that shapes a "show don't tell" culture of excellence, with Olympic medal winners often serving on staff as real consultants, not merely as spokespeople. Second, by choice it focuses exclusively on Netherlands-based clients with the goal of being the best (not the biggest) provider of legal, financial, IT, and human resource consultancy services. Finally, it has wholly adopted business model thinking at the personal, team, and enterprise levels. EIFFEL's commitment to business modeling, design principles, and visual thinking is symbolized by the giant Business Model Canvas adorning its headquarters entryway.

When EIFFEL posted losses for fiscal 2011, management decided the company needed employees to become more

conscious about adding value. "We wanted a workforce that understood the things we wanted to achieve with our customers—people who could place themselves in the big EIFFEL picture and understand which building blocks they would influence," says EIFFEL Senior Marketing Strategy Consultant Dennis Daems. "The financial and euro crisis was a tipping point that made us realize it was the right thing to do."

In 2012, EIFFEL started training all 500 employees, from receptionists to top-level consultants, in the Business Model You® method. Employees came to headquarters in groups of eighteen for full-day sessions. The work took three months to complete.

The training deepened employee understanding of EIFFEL's enterprise model and helped refine their personal business models within the organization: how they create value for EIFFEL and its customers.

"We are convinced we have to offer people the freedom to use their strengths as much as possible," says Dennis. "This inspiration comes from professional sports, where this is the normal approach. You have to get into a position you are good at. We discovered a lot of strengths—and business opportunities—in those sessions."

BUSINESS CONSULTANCY

164

Recruiting and Onboarding

Later that year EIFFEL started to attract new employees by giving applicants a training opportunity that enabled them to create their own personal business models—whether they were hired or not. New graduates were invited to EIFFEL headquarters, trained in the Business Model You® methodology, then invited to create their own personal business models. Those who stood out and showed a clear affinity with EIFFEL's enterprise model were invited by recruiters to join the company. "We still do these workshops to attract new employees, often together with Gold Medalist Ranomi Kromowidjojo or Gold Medalist Pieter van den Hoogenband," says Dennis.

How to Recruit the EIFFEL Way

First, says Dennis, identify the areas where you need help (project management, finance, IT, etc.) and experience levels desired (junior, mid-level, senior). Then, create a recruiting event using EventBrite, Amiando, or a similar service. Consider engaging a friendly and compatible thought leader in your industry to present at the event. Find a meeting venue with plenty of wall space on which to place Canvases. Next, seek out likely candidates via LinkedIn or comparable services. Invite them repeatedly. Here is a typical event agenda EIFFEL uses:

Topic	Time needed (minutes)	Content
Enterprise Business Model Overview	30	Spokesperson presents overview of the enterprise Canvas, uses it to illustrate organization's business model. Invites questions and comments from participants.
Stories from the Learning Edge	30	Thought leader shares stories of recent industry or career-related developments in area of specialty, invites questions and comments.
Personal Business Model Overview	20	Trainer presents overview of Personal Business Model Canvas, invites questions and comments.
Define Your Personal Model	45-90	Trainer asks participants to draw Personal Business Models of roles they believe they can play in your organization. Trainer, other staff may circulate to answer questions. As people complete their models, they move on to "speed-date" individually with a waiting recruiter.
Speed Dating	45-90	Each participant gets five minutes to present their model one-on-one to a recruiter. Recruiter then conducts a brief interview based on the presentation. Another option: Recruiter can share a pre-drawn Personal Business Model Canvas of the way your organization sees a particular open position, have interviewees compare it with their own, and discuss differences.

Interviewees who perform well and whose Personal Business Models resonate strongly with your organizational model can be invited back for a second round of interviews.

Using Personal Business Models for Professional Development

EIFFEL also began using personal business modeling for professional development. Employees start by diagramming their "as-is" personal business models (Point A). Next, they diagram aspirational "to-be" personal business models (Point B). This creates a clear professional development goal: moving from Point A to Point B. But EIFFEL quickly discovered that many employees struggled to discern a specific path for traveling between Point A and Point B. Dennis decided to research professional development plans (PDPs) used by other organizations. He was shocked by what he found.

"Most PDPs are like business plans: lots of text, no visuals, completely impersonal, lacking simplicity and dynamics," he says. "We all know the truth about written plans: nobody reads them and nobody can remember them!" Dennis also felt PDPs were somehow incomplete. So, building on the Personal Business Model Canvas, he created and tested a Personal Strategy Canvas to give employees specific ways to transition from Point A to Point B.

The Personal Strategy Canvas

The Personal Strategy Canvas uses six building blocks to lay out the actions necessary to transition to a new Personal Business Model. Users fill in each block to identify specific actions needed to navigate to their future, "to-be" Personal Business Model. Here is how to do it, illustrated with the example of Karen, an EIFFEL account manager who wanted to transition into consulting:

Knowledge

Describe new knowledge needed to transition to your next Personal Business Model. Evaluate your "to-be" knowledge requirements. Will you need formal accreditation (a degree or certificate)? Will you need to understand concepts that can be learned through courses, books, TED talks, or webinars? If you want to be a salesperson, for example, you will need knowledge about the psychological aspects of the sales process, plus information on the services or products you will sell, the markets you will be in, and the competition you will face. Karen, for example, recognized she needed to learn more about consulting basics, so she created a reading list and signed up for a Service Design Thinking course.

Skills & Abilities

What skills and abilities does your "to-be" model require? List them here. Remember: skills are learned or acquired talents, whereas abilities are natural, innate talents—things you do easily or effortlessly. New abilities are harder to acquire than new skills, so consider whether abilities required by your "to-be" model are within your grasp. The quickest way to acquire or improve skills is on-the-job practice—stretching yourself on the actual "learning edge."

"But do it in a smart way," says Dennis. "If you are an aspiring salesperson, the key is to put yourself in situations where you have to sell something. If you cannot do it at work, try

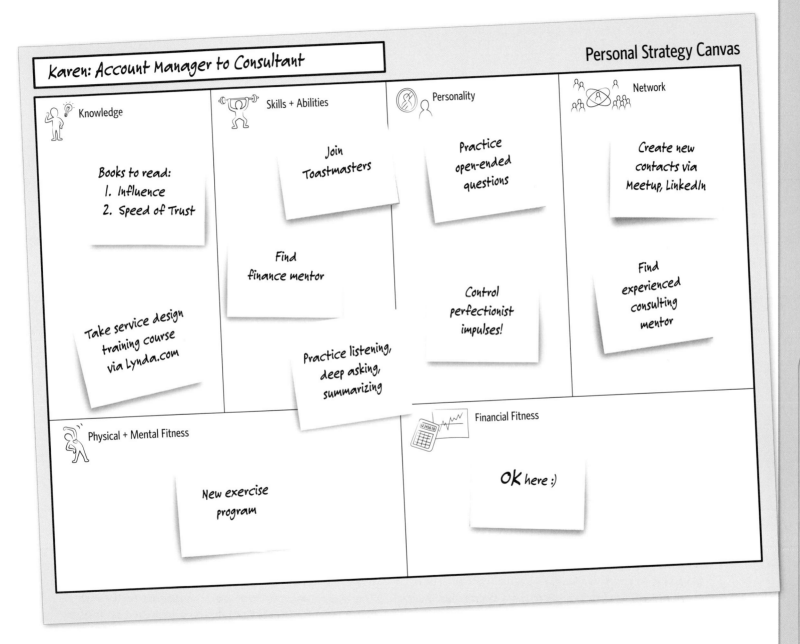

your personal environment. Sell lottery tickets for a school fundraiser or tickets to your tennis club tournament. Put yourself in a position where you grow your experience."

Karen, the aspiring consultant, saw she needed better formal presentation skills, so she joined Toastmasters International. She also found a mentor within EIFFEL who let her sharpen her finance skills by creating some pro forma client engagement estimates in Excel.

Personality

"Everyone has personality traits that help them reach their goals—or not!" says Dennis. "We are not perfect." This building block is all about muting or amplifying certain aspects of your personality to speed progress toward your "to-be" Personal Business Model.

"Most adults who are honest with themselves understand their strengths and weaknesses," says Dennis. "The key is to identify personality strengths that will help you reach your goal, and let those strengths become amplifiers of your development. If you are a very organized person, for example, organize and structure your learning and experiences in detail." Conversely, identify personality aspects that constrain your development, says Dennis. "If you tend to procrastinate, for example, 'mute' that tendency with a countermeasure such as having somebody else push or remind you, or rewarding yourself for completing actions on time," he says. For example, Karen recognized her perfectionist tendency served her well in creating a detailed Personal Strategy Canvas and personal development schedule. At the same time, she strove to tone down her tendency to

ask closed questions and started deliberately practicing open-ended questions in conversation each day.

Mental & Physical Fitness

Mental or physical problems—such as being overweight, under too much stress, or involved in a poor personal relationship—can slow anyone's development. Describe any mental or physical problems you have in this building block, and list actions for overcoming them. Karen knew that she needed to improve her personal fitness. As an account manager, her work was largely sedentary. But as a consultant, she knew she would spend far more time on-site with clients, and would need more energy and physical poise. So she committed to a modest but consistent exercise regime each morning.

Financial Fitness

Money worries thwart effectiveness. If your income is too low or you have excessive debt, take action! Some employers offer help through confidential employee assistance services. You could also try an outside counseling agency, or negotiate compensation with your boss. Financial fitness is essential for stepping up to your "to-be" model—and it will improve even more as you work on the upper building blocks.

Network

This is the most important building block of all, and one you are unlikely to see in any Professional Development Plan. Use it to describe ways to connect to new individuals or groups of people. "We live in a connected, fast-moving, hyper-developing world," says Dennis, "and when you want to be somewhere

Business Model Canvas wall

else, your network has to change. It will change—and it will change you." If you want to become a lawyer, for instance, start getting to know lawyers. Speeding the journey to your next-generation Personal Business Model means entering networks that:

- Give you knowledge in the quickest possible way
- Help you develop skills and abilities in the most effective way
- Amplify or mute your personality in the right areas
- Place you in the context of your to-be model (most new work is won via networking rather than through formal applications)

Your new network connections can be private as well as professional. And meeting new people often helps overcome challenges in the base building blocks: mental, physical, and financial fitness. Where can you find help-giving networks to serve as a bridge to your "to-be" Personal Business Model? That is for you to rethink and discover. Karen joined Meetup and LinkedIn groups and met a consultant nearing retirement who broadened her professional circles and became a strong mentor.

"Every employee on our campus with less than one year of experience has to draw this Personal Strategy Canvas, and has opportunities to review it with a coach, and review other employees' Personal Strategy Canvases as a coach," says Dennis. "Development is not solely about getting a formal promotion—it is about becoming better in your profession. Organizations are getting flatter, which means growth occurs in professions instead of positions."

Results: Improved Retention, Customer Experience
EIFFEL's Net Promoter Score, a measure of customer satisfaction, has improved 20 percent since the company began har-

monizing personal, group, and enterprise business models, according to Dennis. Meanwhile, employee turnover dropped six percent.

The company has also returned to posting solid earnings. The improvements owe to employees becoming more self-directed and better engaged, Dennis believes. "They get it," he says. "They are very conscious that they are driving their own careers."

The Downside?
"Business model thinking is not for everyone," says Dennis. "I always tell my candidates that it is like buying a coat. If it fits, use it. If it does not fit, discard it and find one that does. But this model is the language we use. So you have to learn it if you want to play on our team."

EIFFEL takes a very different approach to human resource work: one that makes employees responsible for defining how they will contribute to team efforts—and how they will develop themselves along the way. Now, the world's largest professional services firm, Pricewaterhouse Coopers (PwC), is experimenting along the same lines. The next case takes an inside look at PwC's mission to reinvent the traditional world of human resource management.

Reinventing Human Resource Management

Riccardo Donelli

"Having employees define their own contributions is a tough path, but it has the potential to unleash tremendous positive energy and generate powerful competitive advantage," says Riccardo Donelli, a 46-year-old senior human resources expert who works for the People & Organisation Services group within PricewaterhouseCoopers Advisory (PwC). "That is why I was convinced that business modeling could shape a new way of managing teams, and ultimately improve the willingness of people to stay, as opposed to just boosting salary or other 'hard' benefits."

Riccardo is on a mission to reinvent the traditional world of human resource management. And he is convinced that the first step is to try new methods in-house.

After becoming intrigued with the idea of using business models in human resource work, Riccardo decided to test the process at PwC with his own group of 25 human resource consultants. His dual goals: 1) assess the method's potential for use with PwC clients, and 2) improve his own team's satisfaction and performance—especially with respect to employee engagement and retention.

"Consulting is extremely competitive in terms of attracting and retaining talented people," Riccardo explains. "Every

day Deloitte, EY, KPMG, PwC, and Accenture all try to steal good consultants from each other. It is a tough market, and salary is only one factor. I believe we need to understand the individual perspective and make people realize that here at PwC, a person can enjoy space for developing what is personally important to them.

"When it comes to people and careers, every day we experience the meaning of the 'digital revolution.' This revolution starts with people, from the bottom up. It has little to do with the traditional top-down way of defining a human resource strategy, then deploying a change management program. People have access to all the information they need for developing their careers, and they enjoy no-cost tools that enable them to navigate and give meaning to this information—and connect with each other.

"This enables people of all ages and types to access more opportunities and better shape their own lives, both professionally and personally.

"More and more, this means that careers are, and should be, designed by individuals who set their own professional and personal development goals, regardless of what the organization has designed for them. As an individual, I will choose the workplace that offers me the best range of opportunities that fit my personal goals."

"This means that companies—and consulting firms are a very good example—should completely redesign their approach to career management, shifting from structured, top-down career paths to flexible opportunities.

"This viewpoint suggests a different relationship between individuals and the organization. We could call it a 'flipped' relationship in that it must start with the organization accepting and responding positively to individual goals—even if those goals might ultimately lead to leaving the organization—and providing more opportunities to achieve those goals in harmony with the organization's strategy."

Riccardo set aside one-and-a-half days to introduce his team of consultants to personal and team business models. He organized the training into four chunks:

1. Draw personal business models (*me*)
Following an introduction to business modeling, consultants drew their own "as-is" and "to-be" Personal Business Models, with Riccardo encouraging them to draw their models freely and include personal goals. Then, he asked them to form groups of three, and coach each other on "as-is" pain points and "to-be" goals. Each participant served alternately as coach, coachee, and observer.

2. Move from individual to team perspective (*me* to *we*)
Riccardo introduced the People & Organization team model and the Alignment Canvas. He then asked participants to juxtapose their personal models on the team model, and for each building block identify how they contribute to group models. Finally, he asked them to assess the alignment between their personal model and the team model. Did their willingness to do things—and their willingness to improve things—match what the organization was asking them to do? If not, how might they change? How might the organization change?

3. Outline personal strategy
Riccardo introduced the Personal Strategy Canvas (page 167), then asked participants to fill it out and include actions PwC could take to help them achieve their goals.

4. Propose specific changes
The participants came up with four initiatives related to either 1) improving workplace life, or 2) boosting team competitiveness, profitability, and staffing effectiveness. Next, they broke into four groups, fleshed out and prioritized rough actions for each initiative, then selected and started working on the one they voted most valuable.

Immediate Results

The business model sessions took place on a Thursday and Friday. By the following Monday, Riccardo and his team had already implemented one of the initiatives. The difference at the Monday meeting was clear, says Riccardo. The group's mood was bright as they took a new approach to the activity they had selected for change: weekly staffing and planning.

"Staffing and planning is a critical business process for a consulting firm," Riccardo explains. "You have several projects going on simultaneously, and you have to constantly assign people to different projects based on their skills and availability, a project's priority at any given moment, its location and logistics, and other factors. This is a complex, cumbersome process that is always a mess at every consultancy, because precise or mathematical upfront planning is impossible.

"What came out of our sessions was that staffing was a painful process for everyone, junior and senior consultants alike. They felt like they were being moved like packages from one project to another without understanding the reasons why. Of course there are reasons, but they are not easy to understand. Our regular Monday staffing meeting process was not working well."

Staffing and planning posed another dilemma: should it be done top-down or bottom-up?

"Top-down is easy, because I can just decide and give orders," says Riccardo. "But I cannot always have all the information at hand or know the critical facts about every project, and scheduling needs to be done every single week. So bottom-up is better. But bottom-up can lead to endless discussions between project managers. This very practical, business-relevant issue came out strongly and clearly during the personal modeling session. So the team decided to identify one coordinator for the process, the tools to be used, the information to be shared, and the key priorities to be applied."

The personal business modeling sessions brought the core problem into sharp focus: a high personal cost in personal and family time. "Everyone, from most junior to most senior, identified this as a problem," says Riccardo. "Everyone said, 'I would like more time for myself.' And as we discussed this during the personal modeling session, everyone agreed that creating more time for themselves depended largely on more efficient staffing and planning. Our current staffing process was costing everybody precious time. We became aware that people were not fighting over staffing issues for arbitrary reasons; everyone was in the same situation."

Here is where Riccardo experienced the power of personal modeling to boost team performance. "All four initiatives started from the personal business model perspective," he says.

"The value of the *me* and *we* modeling sessions lay in establishing a different relationship between individuals, the group, and the organization. It helped reinforce the idea that everyone can and should be entrepreneurial in setting their own goals and strategies for reaching them, but also the fact that this specific organization—and this team—may be the best possible place for reaching them."

What do consultants working for the world's largest professional services firm think of the approach?

"All my people are human resource professionals whose job is to consult with human resource directors about these things. So they know what they are talking about," says Riccardo. "Basically, all 25 participants said this could be a very good service, something we could offer. It was a big organizational 'aha!' for us."

Lessons Riccardo Learned

- Mature adults can figure out what is wrong and collectively decide what to do about it. Let them.
- A day-and-a-half for the initial work was not enough. "I should have planned on at least two or probably three days," says Riccardo.

Things to Try on Monday Morning

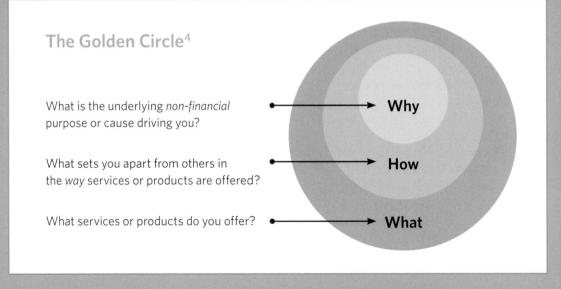

The Golden Circle[4]

What is the underlying *non-financial* purpose or cause driving you? → **Why**

What sets you apart from others in the *way* services or products are offered? → **How**

What services or products do you offer? → **What**

Define the Why[5]

Here is a real challenge: use the table below to define the *what, how,* and *why* for your enterprise, team, and yourself. Your team and enterprise *what* should be easy: these are services and/or products offered. The *how* should be straightforward as well: your business model shows how services and/or products are delivered. But the *why* can be tough. Hint: Describe your enterprise Value Proposition. How does it relate to the reason your organization exists?

	Enterprise	Team	You
What			
How			
Why			

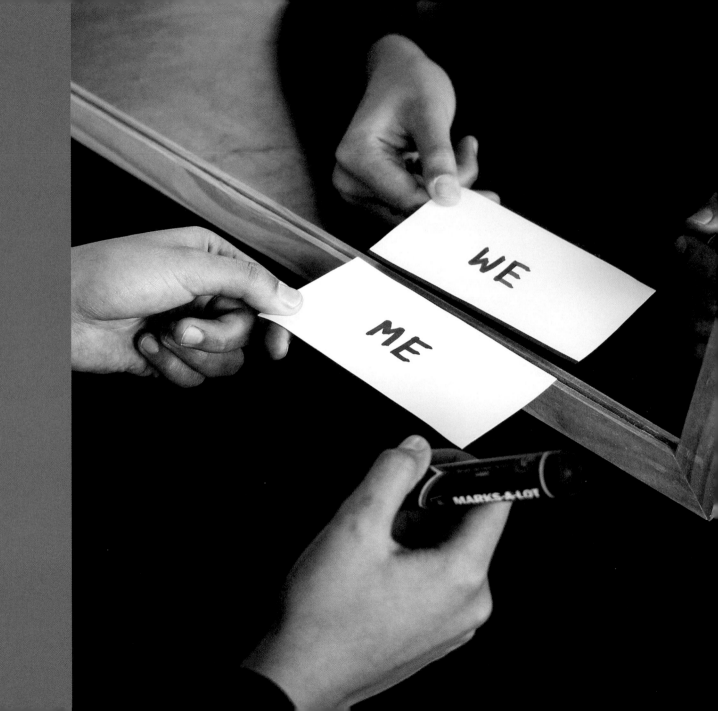

Next Steps

In this chapter you saw how three different organizations aligned personal (*me*) business models with team (*we*) models, enabling group growth and better individual self-direction. Be sure to capture some hands-on learning for yourself by doing the *Things to Try on Monday Morning* exercise.

Next steps: in Chapter 7, learn how Spartan Specialty Fabrications, a midsize leader in a traditional industry, strove to align its teams while battling common events that disrupt personal, team, or enterprise business models. These disruptors will sound familiar—you have probably experienced at least one of them yourself!

You will meet Lianne, and discover how her team, her colleagues' teams, and Spartan itself struggled to align *we* to *we*—and together, how they built a better enterprise.

Align *We* to *We*

The following case illustrates how tools described in previous chapters were used to solve tough workplace problems.[1] Note how business models were used, not to reconfigure strategy, but to 1) clarify what teams do and why, and 2) ensure that the work itself, rather than personality or politics, guided people's behavior.

The Mentor

"Here's my new card, Lianne. Happy to help out anytime. Glad I'm staying on as an internal consultant for a while. Not sure what I'd do as a retiree." The older man laughed as he sipped his espresso.

Lianne Amsden took the card. It read:

SPARTAN SPECIALTY FABRICATIONS

Boris Latchaw
Internal Consultant

"Well, thanks again, Boris. I wish you were still my boss. See you on Monday!" Lianne slipped the card into her bag, replaced her cup, paid the bill, and walked to her car. As she pulled out of the coffee shop parking lot, she suddenly spun the wheel right instead of left. *Given the earnings I bring in, Spartan can afford to let me go home an hour early*, she thought. During the 20-minute drive home, she pondered Boris's advice—and her own future with her employer: Spartan Specialty Fabrications.

Spartan Specialty Fabrications was a century-old "metal-banger" company, as Boris and the old-timers liked to say. The firm built massive, customized iron and steel structures: marine bulkheads, bridge spans, 20-meter high containment vessels for nuclear power plants, meter-thick missile silo doors, and other components demanding unique combinations of precision, quality, and size. Lianne was a rarity in this world: a woman engineer who could talk shop with welders in the morning and present to Nuclear Regulatory Agency inspectors in the afternoon.

Early in her career as a mechanical engineer with the Port Authority, Lianne had become fascinated with massive bridge and bulwark components. Several years later she joined Spartan, one of the vendors she had overseen as a Port Authority inspector. She first worked in Spartan's shipbuilding division, then in commercial fabrication, then with a new team devoted to making components for the regulation-heavy nuclear power industry. That is when Boris Latchaw became her boss. Boris became Lianne's mentor and a welcome advocate for her progress within Spartan's testosterone-fueled culture—until health concerns forced him to consider retiring. Fortunately, Spartan's CEO had persuaded Boris to stay on for another year as a roving internal consultant.

That is when Lianne took over leadership of the nuclear division. And that is when the trouble started.

The Reorganization

Boris had started Spartan's nuclear business as a small, specialized "product team" reporting directly to the CEO. After Boris hired Lianne, sales jumped, thanks in large part to Lianne's extensive regulatory expertise. So when health problems forced Boris to take a six-month leave of absence, he pushed for Lianne to take over the nuclear team—and become Spartan's first woman manager.

Other Spartan executives argued—correctly—that Lianne lacked leadership experience beyond project management. These executives included general manager Damian Glynn, who also led Spartan's Commercial Fabrication business unit. Commercial Fabrication served infrastructure builders by constructing everything from bridge components to oil rigs.

In the end, Lianne was promoted to manager of the nuclear team. But in a nod to those who felt she needed more leadership experience, her nuclear team was made into a sub-team reporting to Damian's Commercial Fabrication division.

The logic was twofold: 1) Damian would provide extensive fabrication leadership experience, and 2) Nuclear was similar to the Defense group—another team with a highly uniform Customer base—which also reported to Commercial Fabrication. The reorganization made sense on paper. But in practice, it was a mess.

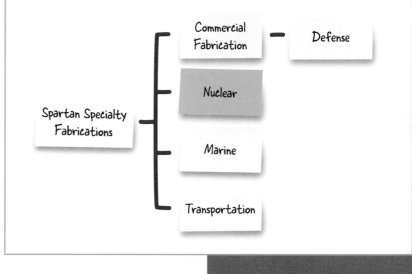

Nuclear started as a standalone product team . . .

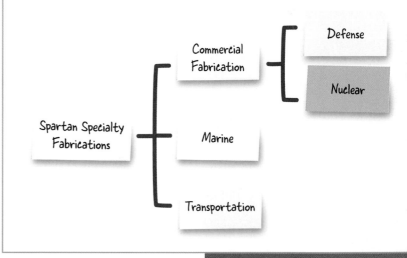

. . . then was repositioned as a Commercial Fabrication sub-team

Heavy Metal Meets New Wave

Lianne had vivid memories of poorly executed performance reviews from her previous managers—when they bothered to conduct reviews at all. Boris had been the single exception.

Now a manager herself, Lianne was determined to do better. She had stayed late for weeks (and even a Saturday or two) to make sure all her direct reports had one-on-one meetings and comprehensive performance evaluations completed by the February deadline. At the last management meeting, she quietly but proudly announced completion of this important work: right after Damian, the meeting chair, reported that none of his own reviews were complete.

Damian reacted to Lianne's accomplishment with all-too-familiar dismissive humor. "Well, I guess some people don't have enough *real* work to do!" he said, drawing a few chuckles from other attendees. Lianne unthinkingly slammed her hand to the conference table and gritted her teeth. But she managed to keep herself from making a caustic reply.

"That cowboy Damian drives me nuts," she later complained to Boris. "If he puts his snakeskin boots up on a table one more time, I'm going to . . ."

Boris interrupted. "Steady, partner! Plain talk with your own staff worked. Couldn't you use that same spirit to 'manage up' and speak one-on-one with Damian?"

"I tried," Lianne replied. "He said I don't understand how Commercial Fabrication runs, or the way Spartan's business works outside of my 'unique little nuclear world.' I reminded him that our team generates better earnings than any other unit at Spartan. That killed the conversation."

Boris looked thoughtful for a moment. Then he spoke. "Lianne, I think it's time for you to *adapt your style.*"

Three Questions for Lianne

"You've made some strong work accomplishments," Boris began. "But they're mostly about managing *down:* leading the people who report to you directly." The older man explained the Three Questions and asked Lianne to describe how each was relevant to her situation:

1. Time to Move Up? *No.* Her latest role as the Nuclear team manager was a well-deserved promotion, and her former boss-turned-advisor believed she could handle it. But the dysfunctional relationship with Damian, her new manager, demanded that she address the third question.

2. Time to Move Out? *No.* Lianne had considered quitting, but leaving Spartan did not feel right. She felt committed to her team and to the important work they were known for delivering.

3. Time to Adapt Style? *Yes.* Lianne had the skills, knowledge, and ability needed for success in her new leadership role. But her delivery style was falling short. "Now, it's time for you to *adapt your style* so you can build greater capacity for *managing up,*" said Boris. "Your leadership challenge is less about producing results and more about aligning your team with other teams—and the enterprise."

Boris explained the five-stage career model and noted that Lianne began, as most leaders do, by testing her training. Then she developed a specialty and a good reputation based on strengths in fabrication processes, production planning, and regulatory affairs. But now she was in stage three: she had jumped to *leading* her specialty. Yet her professional identity remained tightly bound to engineering.

Boris suggested that Lianne expand her professional identity to include leadership. An exercise he suggested provoked an "aha" moment. When pushed to think beyond her job description, she and Boris recognized her strengths as a systems thinker: a strong capacity to see and connect the dots in complex situations—and offer logical, collaborative ideas.

"If you combine this capacity with business modeling," said Boris, "you'll see the bigger picture here at Spartan—and be able to do something about it."

"I'm ready to learn," said Lianne. "How about another mentoring session tomorrow?"

1Q

Is it time to
Move Up?

2Q

Is it time to
Move Out?

3Q

Is it time to
Adapt Your Style?

Business Model Basics

The next day, Boris demonstrated enterprise, team, and personal business model basics, then helped Lianne draw the Nuclear team model. The insights flowed as she saw how the nine Canvas elements were interrelated. "This lets us visualize how we operate as a business within a business," she said. "I'm going to ask my team to diagram our model."

Two days later found Lianne and four of her staff busy working with oversized Canvas posters in a conference room, diagramming "as is" and "to be" models of the Nuclear team. "This is great stuff!" exclaimed a senior project director, after the colleagues had spent nearly three hours diagramming and discussing their team business model. "I've worked here for eight years and managed projects worth tens of millions of dollars. But no one ever explained our business model to me. Why did this take so long?"

"I know what you mean," Lianne sighed. "But insights take as long as they take. Let's list up what we've learned from analyzing our team model." She stepped to a whiteboard, grabbed some colored markers, and wrote down points as her colleagues called them out.

"I'm going to share this with upper management and open some eyes and ears!" Lianne exclaimed as the meeting disbanded. She felt more excited about work than she had in months. Determined to win support for her nuclear team's "to be" model, she immediately called Damian's secretary and scheduled a meeting.

But her meeting with Damian flopped.

Building Block	Notes on "as is" Model	Notes on "to be" Model
Value Proposition	Value Proposition: We "deliver on time and as promised." That's Activity any vendor offers, not Value	We build reputations: our Customers boost their own credibility by listing us as a fabricator in their proposals
Customers	Vague concept of internal Customers, Value Proposition to Spartan undefined	Spartan recognized as our most important Customer. Our Value Proposition to Spartan is big earnings
Key Resources	Over-reliance on a few managers with regulatory expertise	Need more and broader training in regulatory/safety affairs
Costs	Constant pressure/worry over high compliance (administration) costs	Compliance is a key source of reputation and earnings, not "administration." It needs even more investment!
Key Partners	Independent thinking, heroic "go-it-alone" attitude, reluctance to use outside partners	Interdependent thinking, collaborative "we need some help" attitude, more use of outside partners

Business Model Disruptors

Lianne confessed her debacle to Boris at their next mentoring session. "I had the model refined and explained everything. But in minutes he was looking at his phone and glancing at the clock," she lamented. "Maybe I overwhelmed him with too much information and not enough context."

"Exactly, Lianne. Your intent was good and your model well described. But what do you think about the timing with Damian?"

Lianne thought for a moment. "It was all wrong. I jumped the gun. I tried to engage him before he had any background with business models. I was only talking about my team, not the relationship to his. He didn't see the need. To him and his cowboy boots, it was just another annoyance."

"Remember, you spent hours learning with me," said Boris. "Damian is like everyone else. He needs to learn business model basics first, not just see it being used by someone else." Boris paused. "Maybe it would help to consider five common business model disruptors." He walked to the whiteboard and wrote the following five phrases:

- Developmental shifts
  (adapting to growth, decline, change, competition, or innovation)
- Mergers and acquisitions
- New leadership
- Reorganization
- Downsizing

"These five events are red flags signaling that a team or enterprise needs to examine its business model," he said. "What do you notice about this list?"

Lianne thought briefly, then exclaimed, "We're dealing with two of them at once!" Boris smiled knowingly. "Reorganizations and new leadership usually happen at the same time. What have you noticed about Spartan's internal response to these events?"

This time Lianne replied immediately. "No one talks about how a reorganization changes business models. All we got was a new organization chart." She paused. "Metal-banging culture is not introspective. No one wants to talk about what's happening internally. Maybe it's too touchy-feely."

"As my daughter would say, too *emo*," Boris countered.

"Too *girly!*" Lianne shouted. Together, mentor and mentee burst out laughing and were unable to stop for a full minute. The older man regained his composure first.

"So what does all this suggest about how to engage with Damian?" asked Boris. Lianne looked quizzical. "Here's another tool that might help," he said.

Spotting a Gap: Innovate vs. Comply

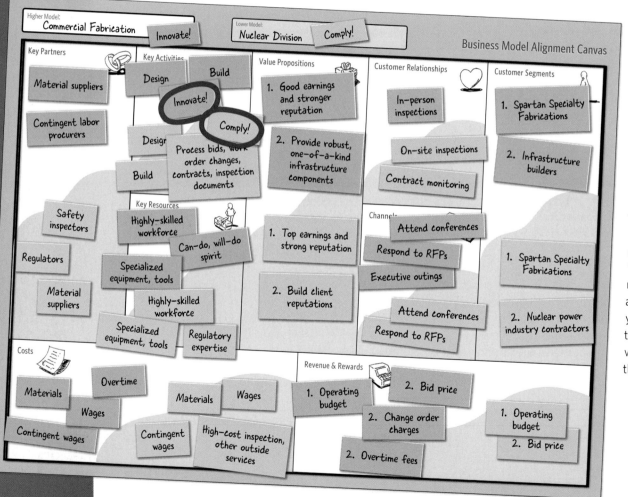

Business Model Alignment Canvas

Higher Model: **Commercial Fabrication** — Innovate!

Lower Model: **Nuclear Division** — Comply!

Key Partners
- Material suppliers
- Contingent labor procurers
- Safety inspectors
- Regulators
- Material suppliers

Key Activities
- Design
- Build
- Innovate!
- Comply!
- Process bids, work order changes, contracts, inspection documents
- Design
- Build

Key Resources
- Highly-skilled workforce
- Can-do, will-do spirit
- Specialized equipment, tools
- Highly-skilled workforce
- Specialized equipment, tools
- Regulatory expertise

Value Propositions
1. Good earnings and stronger reputation
2. Provide robust, one-of-a-kind infrastructure components
1. Top earnings and strong reputation
2. Build client reputations

Customer Relationships
- In-person inspections
- On-site inspections
- Contract monitoring

Channels
- Attend conferences
- Respond to RFPs
- Executive outings
- Attend conferences
- Respond to RFPs

Customer Segments
1. Spartan Specialty Fabrications
2. Infrastructure builders
1. Spartan Specialty Fabrications
2. Nuclear power industry contractors

Costs
- Materials
- Overtime
- Wages
- Contingent wages
- Materials
- Wages
- Contingent wages
- High-cost inspection, other outside services

Revenue & Rewards
1. Operating budget
2. Bid price
2. Change order charges
2. Overtime fees
1. Operating budget
2. Bid price

"This tool juxtaposes two business models to check for alignment—or misalignment," said Boris. He unrolled a poster-sized paper, taped it to the wall of Lianne's office, and explained Alignment Canvas basics. "Now, draw Commercial Fabrication as your higher model, and the Nuclear team as your lower model," the mentor instructed. He sat and watched as Lianne outlined the two models on the poster.

Building Block	Commercial Fabrication	Nuclear Division
Key Activities	(Watchword: Innovate!) Focus on designing and building from scratch	(Watchword: Comply!) Focus on documenting bids, contracts, change orders, inspections, building to plan
Customers	Customers value innovation, speed, and cost-cutting. They are lightly regulated	Customers value compliance, caution, and orthodoxy. They are highly regulated
Revenue	Varies widely with negotiated change order/overtime fees. Based on general estimates	Predictable and reliable revenue stream, based on careful calculations
Costs	Low outside contractor expenses; safety inspectors are already on payroll	High outside contractor expenses; quality inspectors, auditors, specialized engineering consultants are not on payroll
Key Resources	Minimal training needs. Can draw people from other Spartan divisions as needed	Strong need for training in regulatory/safety affairs. No such expertise elsewhere in Spartan

Lianne and Boris compared and contrasted the Commercial Fabrication and Nuclear team business models for a full hour and a half. Then Lianne suggested listing key differences between the two models. Boris walked briskly to the whiteboard and grabbed a black marker. Lianne made observations and Boris wrote them down.

"This is amazing," said Lianne. "And it gives me an idea how I might get Damian on board."

Making the Case with PINT

For months, Lianne had been pushing Damian for approval to hire two additional quality engineers. She requested a three-hour meeting with her boss—and she had to wait two weeks to get one. *But the wait was well worth it,* Lianne thought later.

At the session, Lianne taught Damian Canvas basics, shared her Nuclear team model, then unveiled an Alignment Canvas showing the Commercial Fabrication model juxtaposed with the Nuclear team model. Finally, she unrolled a large, handwritten document. "Boris calls this the Valuable Work Detector," she said. "I just call it the **PINT** tool."

"Well, I must say I'm impressed," Damian admitted when they were done. "I remember the Canvas from an executive MBA class I took a few years back, but thought it was just for startups. And this is my first time with the PINT tool." He looked down at his boots for a moment and hesitated before speaking.

"Listen, Lianne," Damian continued as he looked up, "I've got my hands full running Commercial Fab, overseeing Nuclear and Defense, plus doing general management. Maybe your needs haven't shown up enough on my radar. But you make a good case why Commercial Fab and Nuclear don't align. Feels sort of like a forced fit."

Lianne fought the urge to remind Damian that he had pushed for Nuclear to be under his group. But she saw her opening, and surprised herself with the words that tumbled out. "Well, Damian, let's do something about a situation neither of us likes. How about we present this Alignment Canvas together at the next executive off-site and call for action on it?"

Damian floored Lianne with his quick, positive reply.

"It's a deal," he said.

Problem or Potential

Reorganizations disrupt team business models.
Yet we lacked shared definitions of our team models both before and after the reorganization.
Actions and resources are not ideally aligned.

Needs

Nuclear's recruitment and compensation needs differ from Commercial Fabrication's. For example, Nuclear needs certified quality engineers who are more highly paid than the safety inspectors used by Commercial Fabrication.

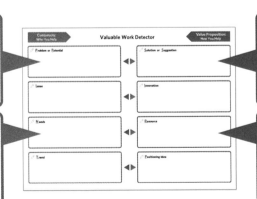

Solution or Suggestion

Collaboratively define and agree on team models everyone can understand and share.
Adjust actions and resources accordingly.

Resource

A different compensation scheme will ensure Nuclear continues to meet its earning goals for Spartan. Success depends on hiring these more expensive professionals.

The Method Acknowledged

A week later, Lianne sat in her office reviewing initial drafts of recruitment advertisements for the new quality engineers. She frowned at the orthodox job descriptions human resources had provided. Then a smile slowly spread across her face as she imagined herself using business models to explain things to promising candidates.

She sketched out a generic personal business model to characterize the new quality engineer role, and became lost in thought imagining new ways such a "role model" might be advertised. *How could we ask applicants to respond? Hmmm...* Suddenly she sensed the presence of another person.

Francis, Spartan's CEO, was standing quietly in her doorway, waiting to be noticed.

Lianne jumped in her chair. "Oh! Hello, Francis."

"Don't get up," the older man said. "I hear you've been stretched pretty thin and just wanted to say 'thanks' for the big effort and good results."

Lianne acknowledged his words with a flushed smile, and Francis let out a booming laugh. "And what's this I hear about the 'modeling' craze you started?' I hope this doesn't mean we all have to start getting dressed up for work!"

"Well, yes!... I mean no... I mean, we've already got some pretty snappy dressers," Lianne stammered, then laughed along with the CEO.

"Anyway, I look forward to your presentation with Damian at the off-site," Francis said. "Just talk with Samantha and let her know how much time you need." Then he was gone.

Lianne could barely contain her excitement. She fumbled for her phone and dropped it. An unintended kick sent it clattering across the floor. Finally, she picked it up and punched a speed-dial number. A moment later a familiar voice answered.

"Boris, it's me!" said Lianne. "Could we move our Friday session to tomorrow? ... Good. And we might have to go longer than usual ..."

Training the Explainers

"Thanks for making time today, Boris." Lianne bustled around her office, clearing papers off her desk and setting out sticky notes, a tape dispenser, and sheets of multicolored sticky dots.

"Glad to," said Boris. "This is a big opportunity. How much time do you have for your session?"

"I've got three hours! One thing I've learned from you—and Damian—is that anything less would just be gesturing at the method. No one would come away understanding how to use it." Lianne finished tidying up, sat down, and faced her mentor.

"Sounds good," said Boris. "How about previewing your session for me? Remember, you'll be training people who will explain modeling to others, including the CEO—the Chief Explaining Officer!"

Lianne settled into the chair, then gave her mentor a thorough overview, jumping up from time to time to point at a flipchart and Canvases. Here and there Boris made a few suggestions. He was clearly pleased with his mentee's knowledge and enthusiasm, especially given that this would be her first management presentation in front of the entire, all-male executive team.

"You're ready," said Boris. "And here are some reminders to pass on to your co-presenter. I don't think Damian is as savvy about teaching as you."

- Think 'touch and go'—show how business models solve problems that personally *touch* people so they'll *go* with you to a new place. Address emotions, not just intellect. "Even cowboys have feelings," Boris said with a wink.
- Avoid extended presentations to a group. Participants should spend most of the time working together in groups.
- Use third objects (Canvases, flipcharts, drawings, sticky notes, etc.) to represent complex systems. Third objects help people avoid abstract discussion and focus on concrete construction.
- Start by practicing one technique at a time. Combining multiple techniques in a single exercise is confusing.

"Thanks, Boris," said Lianne. "Wish me luck."

Breakthrough

At the off-site executive meeting a week later, Lianne opened by defining the term "business model," using the dramatic example of Haloid's invention of the plain-paper dry copier. She then delivered an overview of the Business Model Canvas, and had participants break into teams for a fun but enlightening low-pressure exercise: diagramming the Starbucks business model. Following a break, Damian facilitated team diagramming of Commercial Fabrication's business model.

Lianne introduced the Alignment Canvas and conducted a question-and-answer session. Then, as arranged beforehand, Damian gave a "narrated walking tour" of the Commercial Fabrication portion of the Alignment Canvas, explaining each building block as he placed sticky notes on the paper. Participants nodded their heads as Damian proceeded, for his group was most familiar to them. Even so, they had never seen the business so clearly described. But that clarity was outshone by what they discovered next about the relationship between the Commercial Fabrication and Nuclear Division models.

Lianne started by placing different colored notes on the lower portion of the building blocks repre-senting her Nuclear Division, and telling the story of how her team operated. But midway through her narration, managers began frowning and exchanging quizzical looks, as if to say, "This arrangement makes no sense. Why do things seem so disjointed?"

The questions flew, and Lianne's plans for the rest of this session collapsed in the best possible way. People spontaneously stepped forward to add or remove sticky notes. A spirited discussion overtook the group. No one tracked time. After a while, Francis, the CEO, banged a spoon against a water glass until the room quieted.

"Lianne and Damian have shown us something very important," he said. "For us, business models are not about changing strategy. We are a proven company and we are doing well." The room grew still quieter as Francis faced the two presenters. "But we need a common framework for understanding problems—a more precise way to adjust how we operate. And we need a better way to collaborate. We may have found what we need."

Lianne struggled to keep a modest look on her face. But inside she exulted like a marathon winner.

Realignment

Two months had passed since the executive retreat, and tonight found mentor and mentee together at Lianne's favorite Indian restaurant. "My treat," she had insisted. Boris munched his tandoori chicken as Lianne recounted a series of events at Spartan that had occurred with startling speed, resulting in much-needed relief for both her and Damian.

First, Spartan had created a new business unit called Government Services, reporting directly to the CEO. The new business unit included the Nuclear and Defense teams, and Lianne now served in a dual role: as director of Government Services and leader of the Nuclear team. Her recruitment and hiring needs were addressed with the same consideration given to every other unit within Spartan.

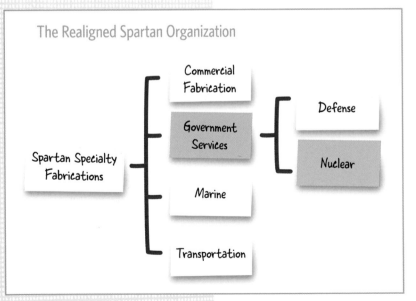

The Realigned Spartan Organization

Second, Francis had taken a keen interest in Lianne's business model initiative. According to Francis, her work was "helping us go beyond our usual opinion-slinging, rambling discussions that trigger more argument than action." In particular, Francis was struck by Lianne's definition of internal Customers, and her appeal that Spartan teams avoid a "false sense of separateness that prevents collaborative action."

Finally, Lianne's relationship with Damian had improved dramatically. He and Lianne were sharing more staff, and collaborating on work to help reduce the extreme revenue swings inherent in Commercial Fabrication's operations. Damian had grown noticeably more polite and respectful to Lianne. And if Lianne was not mistaken, he seemed to have changed his taste in footwear.

"I'm so glad to hear that," Boris said, his satisfaction evident. "I guess my work here is done."

Passing it On

Three days later, as Lianne sat at her desk reviewing finalists for the quality engineer positions, she saw the manager of the Defense team approaching her office. He was smiling and rubbing his hands together like a man about to relish a fine meal.

"OK, I'm ready!" he said.

"For what?"

"I want you to mentor me on getting started with business modeling. I'll start from where I stand. I don't want to wait for Spartan to turn this into a company-wide thing, though I wouldn't be surprised if Francis does just that. I think we've all had our own 'aha' moments, thanks to you. You really let the genie out of the bottle."

Lianne smiled. "I'll be glad to share what worked and what didn't. But first . . ." She opened her desk drawer, rummaged around, then pulled out a business card. "Call Boris. And keep the card. Someday you may pass it on."

Make Things Better

Lianne's experience is one example of using team business models to solve operational problems. But while solving concrete problems, Lianne also started nudging Spartan's workforce toward greater engagement and alignment.

You can do the same thing in your organization. The next chapter shows you how to apply the method, drawing on everything you have learned so far. You will learn a specific process you can adapt to your own needs, illustrated by examples of how leaders in the insurance, software, and technology sectors are using business models to make things better.

Chapter 8

Application Guide

Applying team business models calls for some preparation, but it does not demand a massive, enterprise-wide initiative. This chapter will show you:

- How to prepare to implement team business models
- A step-by-step approach you can adapt to your own needs
- Examples of how three different organizations used team business models to address specific problems

Getting Ready

Before starting, learn from those who have gone before. Here are some hard-won tips based on the successes (and blunders!) experienced by dozens of leaders who have used the methods in organizations ranging from tiny nonprofits to global conglomerates.

Clarify Your Purpose

Be clear about your purpose. Do you want to use business models mainly to solve problems or address opportunities? Or do you want to use business models to start distributing leadership and encouraging self-direction among team members? The first purpose suggests an intervention. The second implies ongoing use and fundamental change. Business modeling is useful for both, and the two often overlap.

Draw Your Own Models First

If you have not yet done so, draw your own personal business model.[1] This will make you familiar with the method and will be tremendously helpful in assessing your current role: are you doing the work you want to at this point in your life? How would you characterize your commitment to your current team and organization? Are you ready to "walk the talk" as the leader of a

business model implementation? These are crucial questions to ask and answer. Then, draw your organization and team models. Are you personally aligned with both? Do not skip this step! You might think, "I get it, and I know what it would tell me," and then avoid actually doing it. But doing it is interesting and instructive—even fun.

Define a Goal, Get Buy-In

Start with the end in mind, as Stephen Covey recommends,[2] and ensure team members agree on the goal. Without participant buy-in, even minor change initiatives are likely to fail. If your aim is to address a specific problem or opportunity, make sure team members agree it is a challenge worth addressing. If you lead a well-functioning team, your goal may simply be to experiment with the method as a new way to train or orient team members, for example. If so, be prepared to accept your experiment's results and take appropriate action.

Find a Thought Partner

Do not work alone! Find a thought partner to help you design and implement. You will need an empathetic colleague, teammate, human resource professional, coach, or consultant to provide objectivity and challenge your thinking. Your thought partner may also implement or train, freeing you to wholly engage in the process as a participant rather than as someone standing apart from your team. However you proceed, having a supportive ally will energize you.

Embrace the "Risk"

It may seem risky for leaders to directly address team and individual purpose with employees. Some managers fear the process will prompt people to leave the organization. Others feel they might "lose control." By this they often mean, *How can I be sure my employees will reach the conclusions I want them to reach?* But let us be honest. *All jobs are temporary.* Employees will leave when they want to leave. If your team or enterprise business model is flawed, why not discover that sooner rather than later? Think of it another way: is it not riskier to *avoid* facing these fundamental issues?

Practice Over Program

As with most new ideas, some colleagues will wait and watch to see if team business modeling is merely a management fad (the latest "pro-gram"). Their skepticism is well justified: up to 70 percent of all organizational change initia-tives fail, according to one prominent leadership consultant.[3] Employee engagement researcher Paul Marciano says people view programs as something done for a limited time rather than as templates for permanent behavior change.[4]

Stay Flexible

Stay flexible. Workplaces are too diverse for one type of implementation to be effective every-where. Remember that tools are simply means for facilitating more potent, meaningful interac-tions between people. Following Canvas guide-lines, for example, is helpful (and sometimes essential to avoid getting bogged down). But do not let guidelines get in the way of your bigger goals. If something is not working, admit it to ev-eryone, and try something else. If you have team members who learn to use modeling very quickly, slow down the learning so others do not fall be-hind in their understanding. Have fast learners coach others and make yourself especially avail-able during the initial learning. One of the extra benefits of learning business modeling together is that it builds team cohesion, joint decision making, and leadership skills.

Birgitte Alstrøm

A Basic Implementation Approach

Once you have completed the basic preparations, it is time to begin. Here is an implementation sequence used by Birgitte Alstrøm, who developed and refined her approach as the leader of a 25-person Web development group at Denmark's national telecommunications carrier.

1. After committing to business modeling in your team, start with the leader

Once you have committed to doing business modeling with your team, start with the leader. If you, your team, your manager, or your organization already have business models in Canvas format, use those in the steps that follow. Few leaders have business model experience, so the rest of these instructions assume you are a leader starting from scratch.

2. Draw your personal and enterprise business models (1-2 hours)

Find a trusted person to coach you through the following process. This could be someone who knows you well, or someone knowledgeable about personal business modeling who can guide and challenge your thinking during the process.

On a clean wall, tape a blank Personal Business Model Canvas to your left and a blank enterprise Business Model Canvas to your right.

Start with the personal Canvas on the left. You can draw both existing and future personal business models on a single Canvas by using different colored sticky notes. Some people prefer to start with their existing personal business model. Others prefer to start by drawing their future personal business model. Take whichever approach energizes you most.

As you go along, draw the enterprise business model on a Canvas to the right (or use an already completed enterprise Canvas). Move back and forth between the personal and enterprise models as you get ideas for each of them. Describe various Customers: your organization, your manager, an internal department, or a paying Customer outside your organization.

Continue until you have completed both your personal Canvas showing existing and future business models, and your organization's enterprise business model.

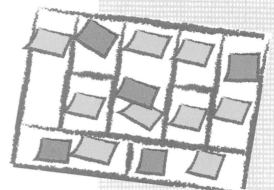

3. Validate the enterprise business model (2 hours)

Present your enterprise Canvas to your own manager, strategy director, CEO, or other person knowledgeable about your organization's strategy. Does your model fit with their understanding of the enterprise model? What modifications are needed?

4. Introduce business modeling to your team, draw your team Business Model Canvas (7 hours)

Plan a training to teach business model principles to your team (if you need help, engage an experienced facilitator to plan and run the training so you can concentrate on experiencing and contributing to the learning outcomes). Show, discuss, and practice drawing various business models before having the team work on your own organization's enterprise Canvas. Next, have participants work on their personal business models. Finally, as a group, draw the team business model. You now have enterprise, team, and personal Canvases that can be aligned.

5. Replace formal professional development with frequent, informal one-on-one discussions

Replace formal professional development efforts with frequent, informal one-on-one discussions with team members. Digital-savvy employees, in particular, seek frequent contact, sincere interest, and commitment from their leaders. Physical presence is not always necessary—you can answer these needs in person or through social media, text, or e-mail. Supplement the informal interactions with regular, half-hour one-on-one meetings, perhaps once every three months. If you feel uncomfortable or need help, engage an experienced coach.

Remember to continuously revisit your own personal business model and discuss it with your own manager, Customers, and partners. When things around you change—or things change for you personally—how will those changes be reflected in your personal model?

6. Improve your model through open dialogue

Improve your team and personal models through open dialogue with team members, Customers, partners, executive staff, and leader colleagues. These dialogues need not be face-to-face or confidential. You now have a tool to tell the story of why you and your team are here. Getting feedback will help you continuously improve.

Brenda Coates

Three Examples of Team Business Modeling

Following are three examples of organizations that used team business models to address problems or potentials, issues, needs, or trends. Note how each organization used several tools covered in previous chapters to identify, characterize, and address different challenges.

Manitoba, Canada–based Protegra describes itself as "a community of software-driven businesses." Protegra operates without managers, emphasizing worker autonomy and self-management in small groups. Co-founded in 1998 by Wadood Ibrahim, the company has employed as many as 78 full-time workers and has twice ranked among Canada's top ten small- and medium-size employers.

Protegra uses business modeling to orient ("on-board") new employees, discover their unseen talents, and help them develop professionally in line with the enterprise model. Here, Protegra's Problem and Needs are described with the Valuable Work Detector.

Problem or Potential

Introverted technical professionals tend to lack a commercial understanding of the business as a whole and the soft skills needed to progress within Protegra

Needs

Technical professionals must participate more as full partners in the business, not just contribute expertise

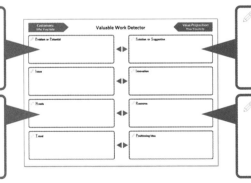

Solution or Suggestion

Have new employees lay out their personal models in the context of the enterprise business model, and chart their own progression through Protegra

Resource

Teach the enterprise model and redefine both individual and team work in terms of Value delivered rather than Activities

Brenda Coates serves as Protegra's Community Lead, the rough equivalent of a human resources executive. On the following pages she describes the role business models play in professional development at Protegra.

Case 1. Reinventing Professional Development at Protegra

Why did Protegra embrace business models so thoroughly?

"Wadood got excited about using the Business Model Canvas because it focuses on *how* we create value rather than *what* we create (the software-enabled solution). When I discovered the personal Canvas, I saw a new way to help our employees develop.

"Protegra employees are 90 percent introverts and many are highly technical. Enterprise modeling helps them think in more business-oriented terms and think of solutions in terms of unstated or non-technical customer needs. Personal business modeling gives them a way to understand interdependencies within teams and the soft skills they need to become more effective and successful.

"At Protegra, we use the Business Model Canvas in strategy development and execution. One of the Canvas's main advantages is it enables collaboration among team members and ensures everyone is on the same page."

How did you go about using personal business modeling at Protegra?

"I started by delivering half-day workshops for ten employees at each session. Then I created a workbook of exercises derived from *Business Model You* and asked employees to work through it on their own time. We ask all new employees to complete our Personal Business Model workbook. I would say about half of our employees are not naturally self-reflective, so this is an important exercise."

Were you concerned that employees who grasped personal business modeling might leave Protegra as a result?

"There was some hesitation about using personal business modeling in-house. Some people thought it might be disruptive. But at the end of the day, we decided we were prepared for people to realize that Protegra was not a good fit and that people might leave. If the tool enables people to realize their calling and it happens to be elsewhere, then this is a good thing since we ultimately helped them pursue what they want.

"There was mixed reaction to the workshops, to be honest. I would say about half of the employees were interested and engaged, the other half less so. Some even complained about the workshop, saying they 'were not looking for a different job'! A few people changed positions within the company as a result of their first encounter with personal business modeling. But no one left."

Using Personal Models as the Basis for Progress

How are the completed workbooks used?

"We use them as the basis for discussion at required individual follow-up sessions. I conduct these together with my colleague John DeWit: One of us acts mainly as a facilitator and the other mainly takes notes. The idea is to give new hires time to get used to the company, then use the Personal Business Model workbook and the private session to find out what they can do beyond what they were hired for."

What do you do during these sessions?

"For one, we have employees use Empathy Maps[5] to describe themselves and gain better insight into their interests, personality, and skills. It is important not to force individual employees to share every aspect of their personal Canvases in a group. Some workbook exercises are very personal, and some people even start crying over things that are not related to work. People are relieved and happy to discover they can bring their whole selves to work."

Describe some results you have seen.

"Ownership and engagement by technical staff has soared. Rather than simply sequencing technical tasks, they now think more about the client's job-to-be-done.

"And people better perceive the value of soft skills. For example, we have one very technical guy who told us he wanted to start serving others as a coach or mentor. Personal business modeling showed him that his Value Provided consisted of technical expertise. *But it also showed him that sheer technical expertise is not enough to attract other employees.* He realized he had to reach out and make himself more personally accessible

A skill identification tool

to others if he wanted to serve as a coach or mentor. I know that sounds like a simple insight, but for someone like him, personal business modeling really drives the point home with strong logic.

"We were surprised to discover that some employees remain hungry for direction. One worker said, 'It's great that we're in a flat organization and enjoy autonomy as employees, but I really need a mission.' Business modeling enables you to define your mission, at the personal or team level.

"Overall, the private sessions have proven exceptionally valuable. They have taught us things about ourselves as an organization that we would not have learned otherwise."

What kind of changes has Protegra undergone as a result?

"Better communication is one—the shared understanding through a common business modeling vocabulary has really helped internal communications. Most Protegrans use the vocabulary. The biggest change, though, is that these individual sessions have largely replaced performance reviews and formal professional development discussions."

Lessons for Leaders

- Using business models is an efficient way to teach the commercial aspects of an organization's operations to highly skilled technical or professional people who may lack commercial savvy or be less customer-oriented.

- Business models show people how to improve by contributing to team goals. Personal model reviews can replace traditional professional development or performance discussions.

- Introducing personal business modeling to an organization is far less risky than it seems. Most people appreciate the opportunity to express their personal aspirations at work.

Luigi Centenaro

Case 2. Sparking Self-Direction at Cattolica

Cattolica Assicurazioni is a century-old Italian insurance carrier that faced a timeless problem: many of its 1,500 employees were not progressing based on their own initiative. Instead, they waited until someone else thought it was a good idea for them to be moved or promoted. Yet faster internal employee mobility was becoming a critical issue for Cattolica due to pressure from nontraditional competitors and tightening regulations. Here are Cattolica's challenges compiled in the Valuable Work Detector:

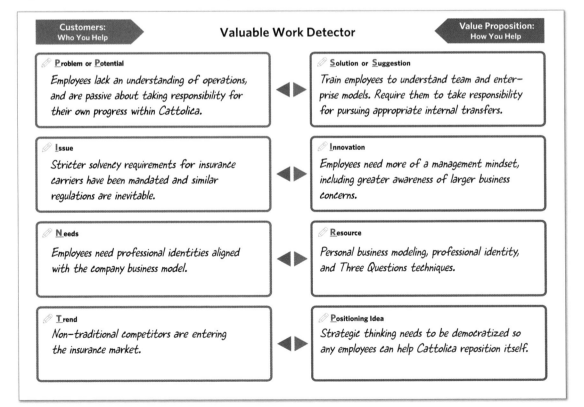

Customers: Who You Help

Valuable Work Detector

Value Proposition: How You Help

Problem or Potential
Employees lack an understanding of operations, and are passive about taking responsibility for their own progress within Cattolica.

Solution or Suggestion
Train employees to understand team and enterprise models. Require them to take responsibility for pursuing appropriate internal transfers.

Issue
Stricter solvency requirements for insurance carriers have been mandated and similar regulations are inevitable.

Innovation
Employees need more of a management mindset, including greater awareness of larger business concerns.

Needs
Employees need professional identities aligned with the company business model.

Resource
Personal business modeling, professional identity, and Three Questions techniques.

Trend
Non-traditional competitors are entering the insurance market.

Positioning Idea
Strategic thinking needs to be democratized so any employees can help Cattolica reposition itself.

Accelerating Internal Mobility

"Eighty employees have requested internal transfers, and some of them have been on the transfer waitlist far too long!" exclaimed Sara Giunta. The 35-year-old training and development manager slammed a thick sheaf of transfer request forms to the table, startling her visitor. "They're burning out, but they're also too passive about changing. Can you help us?"

Luigi Centenaro nodded thoughtfully. Sara's employer, Cattolica Assicurazioni, was Italy's fourth largest insurance carrier. Cattolica's century-long history made it a respected and venerable firm, but one with legacy practices now being challenged by keen competition from nontraditional players. Sara had called on Luigi to help Cattolica develop more agile human resource processes, in particular to spark greater "internal mobility" among its 1,500 employees.

Sarah found a kindred spirit in Luigi, a specialist in people development who used principles of business design. The two agreed that personal business modeling would help Cattolica employees develop what Sara called a crucial "meta-competence": the ability to manage their own careers and engage in more productive dialogue with leaders. Sara agreed to engage Luigi and his team.

During the discovery phase of the work, Luigi and Sara identified the following problems with Cattolica's aspiring transferees:

- They did not fully understand operations, either in their current teams or teams for which they hoped to work
- They were unaware of the value they created, either in current or possible future roles
- They were incapable of identifying, understanding, then positioning themselves to seize opportunities available within Cattolica
- They were unaware of the importance of being able to pitch themselves effectively
- They lacked an understanding of career management and felt little personal responsibility for it

Sara and Luigi agreed to focus on teaching a process and accompanying skills that would enable many of the aspiring transferees to redeploy in new roles within Cattolica. Luigi and his team then designed a series of trainings to teach business model basics and develop among participants a sense of professional identity that would enable them to become more self-directed in whatever work they chose to pursue at Cattolica.

The Training

First, Luigi's team trained human resource and business unit representatives in the basics of personal business modeling. Next, together with Cattolica staff, they agreed on a three-step "pathway" for aspiring transferees: 1) preliminary interviews, 2) training sessions, and 3) follow-up meetings with appropriate human resource or business unit representatives. The goal was to give participants the skills they needed to pursue new professional paths within Cattolica.

The training phase had four components:

1. Team and Enterprise Business Model Basics

Using the Business Model Canvas to better understand Cattolica's overall operations and the operations of current (and potentially future) teams.

2. Professional Identity and Three Questions

Teaching professional identity and Three Questions basics to build awareness of personal responsibility for the upcoming process of shifting to new roles within Cattolica.

3. Personal Business Model Drafting and Alignment

Drafting "as-is" personal business models to better understand current roles and the logic of related roles. Generic personal business models for available positions within Cattolica were then presented so participants could understand well-aligned business roles and their potential fit with those roles.

4. Personal Branding Applied to Target Role

Training participants in personal branding, then having them select one of the positions described in 3) above. Finally, participants discussed and drafted personal development plans, then practiced new self-presentations to be used during follow-up interviews with human resource and business unit leaders.

Results

The trainings were carried out over a period of five months with between 12 and 15 participants in each of six separate sessions. Luigi's team and Sara took a lean approach, emphasizing continuous optimization, monitoring of follow-up interviews, and tracking relocation results. Thankfully, the process was welcomed by Italy's trade unions.

Sara is pleased with the results. "So far, 40 percent of the participants have relocated internally," she says. "That is a big win for Cattolica—and for our employees."

Lessons for Leaders

- A surprising number of employees do not understand how their employer operates. Teaching the enterprise business model is a fast way to build this understanding.

- Leaders cannot impart self-direction—but they can teach specific skills that encourage it.

- Too many employees fail to understand the difference between Activity and Value. Teaching personal and team business modeling is an effective way to create this understanding.

Marco Linde

Case 3. Defining an Employer "Brand" at ANT

Applied New Technologies (ANT), located in the city of Lübeck in northern Germany, is a 26-employee firm and a world leader in its field: designing sophisticated equipment used to eliminate extreme hazards for energy industry clients. Yet ANT was struggling to attract and retain good workers. Like many organizations founded and staffed by highly technical or specialized professionals, ANT lacked insight into what made the firm an attractive employer. To find out, it undertook a comprehensive change initiative based on business models.

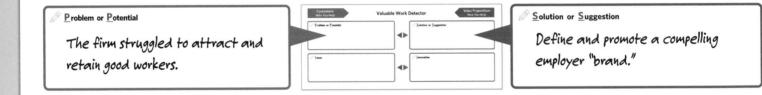

Problem or Potential

The firm struggled to attract and retain good workers.

Solution or Suggestion

Define and promote a compelling employer "brand."

Every Day an Adventure

When the caller said "unexploded bomb," Marco Linde felt a familiar twinge of excitement.

Tackling dangerous, difficult problems was business-as-usual for ANT's 48-year-old COO. Marco had co-founded the firm 20 years earlier, and ever since, clients around the world had relied on him and his team to deliver equipment to safely defuse explosives, remove redundant oil wells located hundreds of feet underwater, and decommission nuclear power plant equipment.

The secret to ANT's success lay in unique water-jet technology that enables sparkless, remote-controlled cutting of super-hard materials used in mission-critical energy and military applications—usually in situations where excessive heat or a single stray spark could trigger disaster.

Every day an adventure, thought Marco, as he hung up the phone. While he relished ANT's problem-solving challenges and life-saving outcomes, on this day he knew he had to address a long-standing, slow-growing leadership challenge: one less exciting than an unexploded bomb, but equally dangerous. *And*, thought Marco with a heavy sigh, *it's a problem I have no idea how to solve.*

Marco's problem was simple: ANT was struggling to attract and retain good workers—and that was beginning to threaten its viability. While the company was a leader in the field of water-jet cutting and enjoyed a strong reputation in the oil, gas, and

nuclear power industries, it had almost no name recognition outside of its highly specialized niche. Few graduates of Lübeck's single engineering school knew of ANT, and like most graduates everywhere, young engineers were eager to move to bigger cities like Hamburg and Stuttgart or seek careers with more visible technology companies such as Siemens, or Dräger, the local technology star.

ANT is truly an 'unknown champion,' thought Marco. Now, the company had reached a turning point. Marco realized it was time for ANT to boost its visibility as an employer or risk decline. But where to start?

Marco turned to Dr. Jutta Hastenrath, an organizational development and human resource consultant with deep experience in both enterprise and personal business modeling. During their first meeting, Jutta asked some basic questions: What kind of workers make ANT's business successful? How do you go about finding them? What makes ANT an attractive employer?

The more Marco and Jutta talked, the more they realized that ANT needed more than just a way to attract and retain good workers: it needed a clear "face" to the world—an employer "brand" true to its internal culture and compelling to prospective hires.

Together, Marco and Jutta agreed to work on a comprehensive set of changes related to ANT's:

- Corporate culture and employer brand
- Methods to recruit, retain, and promote good workers
- Ability to match workers with positions where they could be most effective

Marco, his management team, and Jutta ended up working closely together for more than nine months to design and implement these changes. As she began working with ANT, Jutta quickly discovered that engineering—and engineering alone—drove the company. ANT had grown in lockstep with its customers' unique technical problems, to the extent that most client engagements produced an entirely new ANT product-service offer.

Jutta Hastenrath

Defining an Elusive Culture

Despite their intense focus on technology, ANT employees had forged a unique and highly cohesive team. Many had known each other since the company's founding, and had lived through its ups and downs together. While ANT wanted to hire new people, prospective employees had to fit in to a culture difficult for outsiders to understand. Jutta concluded that to create an employer brand and a good hiring strategy, ANT first needed to define its culture and clarify its business model. She organized her objectives and actions as follows:

Objective	Action
Define strong employer brand	Articulate company culture
Identify skill, competence gaps	Define & share enterprise business model
Devise better recruiting, retention methods	Define personal business models for each job function
Effectively position workers	Use personal business modeling as basis for professional development

Start with Managers

"Some managers fear that if employees recognize new possibilities for themselves, they might decide to leave and seek more attractive work elsewhere," says Jutta. "That is why you need to start with managers. Managers must see the day-to-day value of the method to them personally: how it helps assign tasks to the right team members and improves the overall workplace environment.

"At ANT, we addressed this through 'pre-workshops' for the managers. These took place several weeks before the team and all-employee sessions. We actually rehearsed sessions to test the method and specific exercises with the managers. They experienced it for themselves and discussed the results. Some of them decided then and there to adopt the approach for their employee performance and development discussions."

The Spirit of ANT

Jutta arranged a special culture-defining session in which she asked small groups of employees to tell each other stories about exciting things that had happened at work, or to share jokes they felt colleagues might enjoy. She discovered how closely ANT employees worked together, and how deeply they valued the 'adventure' of collaboratively tackling daunting customer problems. The session produced two phrases that captured the company's internal spirit: *Customer problems are our adventures. We write the history of technology.* Now, it was time to define ANT's business model.

Illuminating a Tacit Model

Visually depicting ANT's business model revealed an important deficiency: the intensive focus on technical solution-building was leaving Customer acquisition to chance. Most new Customers were acquired through recommendations from previous clients. ANT urgently needed an experienced business development professional.

Working off the enterprise model, Jutta and ANT's executive team used personal modeling to create a business development manager profile, focusing sharply on the new position's Value Proposition. Then, they incorporated Jutta's own profiling techniques to develop a detailed job description closely harmonized with ANT's culture. Rather than listing the opening with executive recruiters and on job boards, ANT decided to announce the new position internally—and share it with a few outside partners.

The approach worked. At one of Jutta's public career workshops, an engineer drew a personal business model that happened to closely match ANT's profile. Jutta introduced the engineer to ANT's COO and the two immediately hit it off.

"It was clear to everybody that the personal business model approach was extremely useful in determining fit with company culture," says Jutta. "ANT expressed itself clearly through its enterprise model and the new colleague

profile. For his part, the candidate quickly saw how his own values aligned with ANT's, and was eager to learn more about the company. Their first meeting revealed that talking in personal business model terms works splendidly as a common language for evaluating employer-employee fit."

Since then, ANT has taken the same approach to recruiting, refining the method slightly with each new hire. To attract interns and raise ANT's profile in the community, it customized the process for engineering students at the local university.

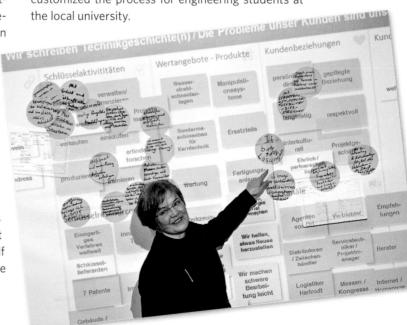

Aligning Individual Actions with Enterprise Aims

ANT management decided to go further, and use business modeling to align individuals actions with company aims. Jutta designed training to integrate the personal business models of all employees into ANT's enterprise model.

Jutta started her first all-employee session by projecting ANT's enterprise Canvas onto a huge screen for everyone to see. Together they discussed new service ideas and the company's future prospects. Thanks to the visual model, everyone could see ANT as a living, interdependent system, where everything was connected to everything else.

"The revenue and expense realities were an eye-opener for many employees," says Jutta. "They saw with their own eyes how new devices alone cannot create a successful business model."

Jutta then asked participants to anonymously identify their individual contributions to ANT's business model by placing stickers in appropriate building blocks. As Jutta expected, no one placed stickers in the Channel building block. Almost all employees identified themselves as either engineering

experts (Key Activities) or technical problem solvers (Customer Relationships). The clustered stickers revealed the true problem: ANT needed marketing links (Channels) to prospective Customers.

To uncover hidden talent that might remedy this, Jutta followed up with a series of in-depth personal business model training sessions.

Connecting Enterprise Understanding to Individual Roles

After introducing the personal business model Canvas, Jutta focused on the concept of Value Proposition, using the example of a new warehouse position ANT wanted to fill. Jutta had participants draw their own "as-is" personal business models, then share their talent profiles and Value Propositions with colleagues.

Next, Jutta asked participants to draw future versions of their personal models, and to place these "to-be" models within ANT's enterprise Canvas. Doing so showed that some employees, indeed, imagined new Customer-related areas of responsibility for themselves. Again, the oversized projection of the enterprise Canvas offered a decisive advantage in letting participants see the "big picture" and visualize future opportunities within the company.

"A number of employees said that, for the first time, they truly understood what ANT was about—and they could imagine promoting ANT job openings to friends and acquaintances," says Jutta.

From Value Proposition to Professional Development

The next step in ANT's quest to burnish its employer brand involved training employees to create their own professional development paths. In a series of separate sessions, Jutta had small teams work on their personal business models in detail. Each employee created an "as-is" Canvas describing their current work, followed by a "to-be" Canvas envisioning a future role. The result, says Jutta, was that "employees created their own professional development plans. The idea was to encourage self-direction and ownership of their own professional progress."

Some workers discovered they needed additional technical training. Others realized they were missing certain leadership skills, or wanted to take on a few supervisory duties to test their appetite for management. Every ANT employee participated in this training—and the result, says Jutta, was a practical development plan for each and every person.

"The company's business model was clear to everyone," says Jutta. "So these development plans became a sound base for subsequent performance discussions between managers and their direct reports."

To keep pace with market changes—and keep its eye on the big picture—ANT plans to hold a yearly "talent and strategy day" to verify alignment between the enterprise and personal models.

ANT's Discoveries

By combining employer branding, people development, and business modeling, ANT created a practical, yet deeply strategic approach to acquiring and integrating new employees, says COO Marco. Now, Marco says, ANT employees are ideal ambassadors for finding new colleagues—and new clients. They understand their employer's Value Proposition and can communicate it clearly and with passion. Plus, they know how to find personal development opportunities within the company, for themselves and for others.

Understanding ANT's needs while simultaneously seeing personal benefits for themselves within the enterprise model strengthens the *we* power—and willingness to promote the company, Jutta adds. Each employee is ANT and part of the ANT business model. Because employees understand their own needs and want to progress toward a "to-be" personal model, they are better able to interact with their supervisors as peers rather than subordinates when discussing personal development, she says.

Lessons for Leaders

- Employer branding is underpinned by culture, and culture defines the team-binding spirit that prospective employees find compelling. As Peter Drucker reportedly said, *culture eats strategy for breakfast.*

- Management concerns about employees leaving should be taken seriously and addressed early. Demonstrate the method to managers first, so they understand that personal business modeling will likely bring employees closer to the organization, not distance them from it.

- The method effectively aligns individual behavior (*me*) and enterprise goals (*we*).

- Seemingly localized operational problems are often symptoms of systemic challenges. When you undertake business modeling, be ready for an adventure!

Things to Try on Monday Morning

Your Launch Brief

It is time for you to start using team business models. Refer back to the Draft Your Team's *Why* Statement on page 17. Then, revisit the Define the *Why* exercise on page 175. After you have thought carefully about those two exercises, jot down your thoughts in the Launch Brief below:

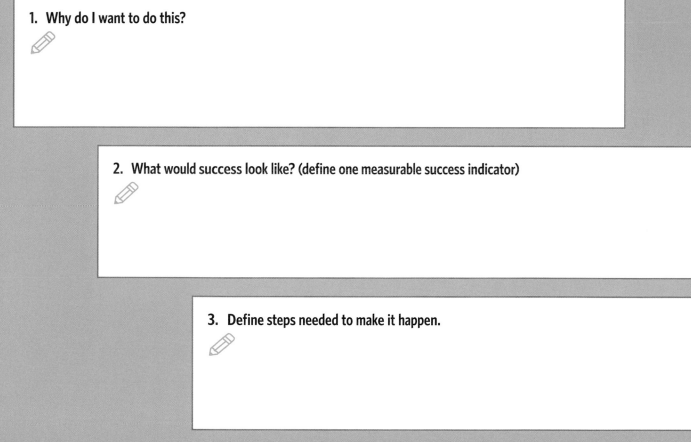

1. **Why do I want to do this?**

2. **What would success look like? (define one measurable success indicator)**

3. **Define steps needed to make it happen.**

4. **When you have worked through your Launch Brief, share it with a thought partner (see page 232) and discuss how to proceed.**

Making It Happen

Everything in the book so far has led to this point: the time to work on your team's business model. If you have completed the Launch Brief on page 221, you are already moving forward and can simply refer back to material in previous chapters as needed.

But if you do not feel quite ready to work on a Launch Brief, continue on to Chapter 9. This final chapter of *Business Models for Teams* briefly reviews five potential stages of a team business modeling initiative, and describes one new exercise or technique that can help at each stage. Here is an overview:

1. Define the Purpose of Modeling
Several exercises in the book can be used to define the purpose of your business modeling initiative. Then, Pre-Briefing can help you virtually "test" the viability of any particular approach to your initiative.

2. Draw the Leader's Personal Business Model
You know the basics of drawing personal business models. Doing the Pair and Share exercise will deepen your understanding of your own model.

3. Draw the Enterprise Model
To prepare to diagram your enterprise model, follow these Tips on Selecting and Briefing a Thought Partner. Then use a Think Out Loud Laboratory to gain a broader (and deeper) perspective on the enterprise model.

4. Train Your Team, Draw Team & Personal Models
Try the Jigsaw exercise: a potent way to generate a "360° view" of your team business model—and win buy-in on its final definition.

5. Discuss and Decide
With your team, discuss the implications of your business model insights and agree what to do. The Fast-Forward the Movie exercise helps move you from agreement on implications to agreement on actions.

Chapter 9

New Ways to Work

1. Define Your Purpose in Modeling

It makes good sense to define the purpose of your business modeling initiative before getting started. So far the book has presented two opportunities to reflect on organizational and team purpose. If you have not yet done so, return to Chapter 1 (page 17) and complete the **Draft Your Team's *Why* Statement.** Then, revisit Chapter 6 (page 175) and try the **Define the *Why*** exercise.

The two exercises are similar. If you complete both—or complete the same exercise on more than one occasion—you may find that your responses differ. This is perfectly normal. Welcome to the world of business modeling! Forget perfection. Instead, strive for a simple, workable *why* definition that helps you and your colleagues.

Now, given your *why* definition, decide on the purpose of your business modeling initiative. Do you need to solve problems? Capitalize on opportunities? Distribute leadership? Encourage self-direction among team members?

Once you feel you have reasonably defined the purpose of your business modeling initiative, you may want to "test" the viability of different approaches to your work. This is where Pre-Briefing can help.

Pre-Briefing

Everyone understands *debriefing* as a good way to learn from hindsight. After completing a piece of work, a team reviews mistakes made, assumptions proven faulty, and so forth, then brainstorms ways similar problems might be prevented next time.

But surely things would have gone better if the team had anticipated those mistakes *before* getting started. That is the idea behind *pre-briefing*, which takes place *before* a project starts. It asks you to imagine the risks, unforeseen events, and missing or careless actions that might combine to cause failure or underperformance.

Conducting a pre-briefing session is simple, and is best done with a thought partner (or the team about to undertake the work). Getting thoughts out of your head and onto paper is an important first step. But sharing your thinking aloud with an empathetic listener(s) will advance your project much farther compared to working solo. So if you have been working on your own, now is the perfect time for you to engage a thought partner (more on this soon).

To start your pre-briefing, simply ask and discuss the question, *What might go wrong?* Voice and list concerns, then rank them in order of risk or likelihood. Finally, determine potential counter-measures. What must go right? Make sure to take and retain good notes!

If you conduct your pre-briefing with a team, you might want to start by soliciting written rather than verbal responses. This gathers more perspectives and helps keep the subsequent discussion from being dominated by the first or most confident speakers. Encourage experience-based comments over formal risk analysis. You could then list the comments, prioritize them, and decide on preventative actions that become part of the work. End on a positive note about the opportunities ahead (and save notes on threats and preventive actions).

A Note on Debriefings

Debriefings are meant to foster continuous improvement. But they are often skipped: sometimes because of pressure to move on, and sometimes because of reluctance to discuss unresolved conflicts that arose during the course of the work. Here is a reality check for leaders: Are you letting relationships suffer in service to the expediency of completing work? If so, you are missing a tremendous learning opportunity—and restraining personal growth for your team and yourself. Once you start doing *pre-briefings*, you will have a new third object tool to use for *debriefings*. At your next debriefing, share your *pre-briefing* disaster scenarios or "what could go wrong" lists, and see which threats were successfully anticipated or avoided. Celebrate your successes!

2. Draw the Leader's Personal Business Model

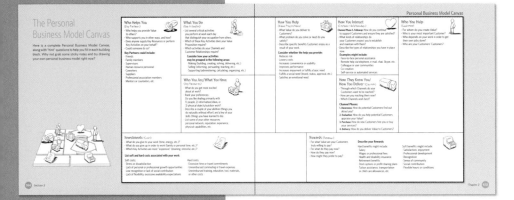

Draw Your Personal Business Model (pages 104–105)

If your business model initiative includes personal business models, it is important for you to use the personal Canvas for yourself. Chapter 4 shows how to draw personal business models. If you have not yet done so, draw your own personal model using the Canvas on page 104. Be sure, too, to try the **Professional Identity** exercise that appears on page 110. Next, examine your personal work style with *Skyle Zones* (page 116) using yourself as the subject. Finally, you may want to try the approach described on page 202, where you simultaneously work on both your personal business model and the enterprise model of your workplace. Drawing your personal model is revealing—often startlingly so. But to progress faster and further, work on your personal model with a partner. The following two-person exercise is ideal for that.

> Step 3. I intuitively uncover hidden stories that demand sharing.
>
> People feel pride and accomplishment when reading what I write about them.
>
> I'm a corporate diplomat who shuttles across organizational borders to produce strategic, sense-making stories.

Professional Identity exercise (page 110)

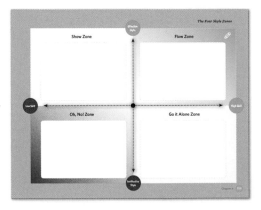

Skyle Zones (page 119)

Pair and Share

The Pair and Share exercise allows two people to help each other use personal business models to clarify their roles and team/organization alignment. Use it with your thought partner to work on your personal business model as a leader (later, you can use Pair and Share with your own team).

☐ **Goal**

Clarify your role and alignment with your team/organization.

☐ **Requirements**

One oversized personal business model Canvas poster each for you and your thought partner, taped to a wall, plus sticky notes in several colors and two black markers.

☐ **Preparation**

Both participants should be familiar with enterprise and personal Canvases, and should have drawn their personal models.

☐ **Procedure**

Decide who will be the client, and stand in front of the client's Canvas. The partner serves as coach.

The client explains their personal business model to the coach. This should be in the form of a concise story that describes mainly Customers, Value Propositions, and Key Partners, and avoids lengthy explanations of Key Activities and other building blocks. The coach should ask clarifying questions until the client's model is well understood.

The coach then asks the key Pair and Share question: "What is the biggest pain point in your model?" The client locates the pain point within a specific building block. The coach then summarizes the pain point on a different colored sticky note, and places that note in the building block where the "pain" resides.

The coach continues to facilitate by asking how the pain point is related to or caused by elements in other building blocks. How might those elements be modified to address the pain? What is the relationship between the pain point(s) and the client's personal alignment with the team or organization? Client and coach should cooperatively write ideas on different colored sticky notes and place them in the appropriate building blocks.

Debrief. Then, switch roles: the coach becomes the client and the client becomes a coach. Repeat the exercise in the new roles, and debrief again.

Modified Pair and Share
for Use with Teams

Here is a modified version of Pair and Share that you can use with teams. The basic idea is to have colleagues help each other rather than take directions or receive feedback from leaders. Peer coaching can be 1) more powerful than leader coaching, 2) a more efficient and engaging way to work, and 3) a potent way to produce behavior-changing experiences.

☐ Room and materials requirements
One oversized personal business model Canvas poster per participant, plus sticky notes in several colors and one black marker per participant. Use a space big enough so that people can comfortably work in pairs with oversized Canvases taped to the walls.

☐ Preparation
All participants should be familiar with enterprise and personal Canvases, and should have drawn their first personal models on Canvases pre-taped to the walls. Pair and Share can be used immediately after participants draw this first version of their personal models. You may find it helpful to project written exercise instructions on a Keynote or PowerPoint slide for reference by participants. Consider limiting the amount of time available for each step of the exercise, and projecting a timer so participants know how much time is left during each step.

☐ **Procedure**

Explain that participants are going to coach each other through a process called Pair and Share. Pair the participants. You can simply have people work with whomever happens to be their neighbor, or you can do some social engineering and decide beforehand who will benefit most by working with whom.

Ask pairs to decide who will be the first client (the other person serves as coach). Have each pair move to the client's Canvas on the wall.

Give the following instruction:

"Clients will now briefly explain their personal business model to coaches. Clients, tell your work story describing mainly Customers and Value Propositions—avoid talking at length about Key Activities and other building blocks. Coaches, ask clarifying questions to make sure you understand the client's model. Then, ask the key Pair and Share question: 'What is biggest *pain point* in your model?' Make sure the client locates the pain within a specific building block. Help them by summarizing the pain in writing on a different colored sticky note, and posting that note in the appropriate building block."

Continue to facilitate:

"Coaches, ask how the pain point is related to or caused by elements in other building blocks. Ask how those elements could be modified to address the pain? What is the relationship between the pain point(s) and alignment with the team or organization? Work with your client to write ideas on different colored sticky notes and place them in the appropriate building blocks."

Ask pairs to switch roles:

The coach becomes the client and the client becomes a coach. Repeat the exercise.

Debrief. Ask participants to share what they discovered, and what actions they might take based on what they learned.

3. Draw the Enterprise Model

When you are ready to diagram your enterprise business model, refer to Chapter 2 and the practice exercise on page 54. Then, try drawing your enterprise model. If you get stuck, seek out examples of similar business models for hints and inspiration. When you feel you have a reasonable enterprise model, it is time to engage a thought partner.

Tips on Selecting and Briefing a Thought Partner

The primary role of a thought partner is to ask questions that will push your thinking beyond what your initial business model reflects. Here are some qualities to look for in a thought partner:

1. Good listener who hears what people are seeking to express beyond the literal meaning of their words
2. Genuinely curious and able to ask open-ended questions rather than judging or critiquing ideas
3. Enjoys a basic understanding of your team and the larger organization; does not need the basics explained
4. Systems thinker who sees the interdependencies in an organization, good familiarity with business models
5. Able to keep confidences about tentative ideas or plans discussed
6. Will push you to be clear and concise

Once you have enlisted a compatible thought partner, use a Think Out Loud Laboratory to gain a broader (and deeper) perspective on your enterprise model.

Think Out Loud Laboratory

Ideally, your thought partner will already be well-versed in business models. If not, be prepared to offer an intensive Canvas training session, using examples of either well-known organizations or organizations similar to yours. Avoid using your own organization to conduct the training—that is a mission-critical task that should be undertaken during the *Think Out Loud Laboratory* session itself. Note: Training this person in business models is an investment that will pay off repeatedly if you serve each other as sounding boards in the future.

☐ **Goal**
Create a workable version of your enterprise business model that can be shared with your team.

☐ **Preparation**
This is similar to Pair and Share, but is designed for two people who have a strong management understanding of the enterprise. Both participants should be familiar with the Canvas approach to business models. Explain to your partner that you need them to provide good questions, summary statements, and observations. Their job is to push your thinking beyond what is possible in the privacy of your own mind.

☐ **Room and Materials**
Find a quiet, private space where you can work without interruption. Tape one oversized enterprise business model Canvas poster to a wall. Have sticky notes in several colors and two black markers available.

☐ **Directions**
Start describing the enterprise model (or the higher model with which your own team will align). Write simple, clear descriptions of building block elements on sticky notes and place them appropriately on the Canvas. As you do so, talk to your partner about your descriptions and why they matter. Your partner's job is to prompt you with statements such as, "Why is that important?" "Say more about that," or "You have just described an activity, not a Value Proposition." Their knowledge of the enterprise will enable them to notice things you may be leaving out or interpreting differently.

Once you have completed the Canvas, take several minutes to "narrate" the model: tell a clear, concise story about whom the enterprise serves and what value it provides. Practice telling this business model story several times, soliciting feedback from your partner each time, until you both feel the story is crisp and compelling, and you can tell it without using distracting filler words such as "um," well," and "you know . . ." One benefit of the Think Out Loud Laboratory lies in allowing you to experiment with and practice the business model story before you meet with others in a situation where you want every word to count.

4. Train Your Team, Draw Team and Personal Models

Everything in *Business Models for Teams* leads to some form of business model training, socialization, or experimentation: each chapter contains techniques, exercises, and tips to help you and your collaborators design and implement a successful business model initiative. Step 4 could be the heart of your initiative: it foresees training your team in business modeling, then having members draw team and personal business models.

The Jigsaw Exercise is a dynamic way to handle team model definition, and offers the side benefit of requiring self-directed behavior. Like a jigsaw puzzle, everyone contributes a piece or two to create the whole picture.

The Jigsaw Exercise

This exercise is meant for leaders who want team members themselves to articulate their team model. Teammates who collectively define and agree on a model are likely to firmly commit to it. Once committed, it is a natural next step for team members to define (or redefine) their personal models in terms of contributions to the agreed-upon team model.

☐ **Goal**
Have team members define and agree on a team business model.

☐ **Room and materials requirements**
One oversized enterprise Canvas poster per 2-3 participants, pre-taped to walls of a room big enough to accommodate the entire group. Separate the Canvases so each group of two or three can work comfortably around their Canvas and move freely around the room to view other Canvases. Provide sticky notes in several colors and one black marker per participant. Projecting a timer is helpful, as is a bell or whistle to signal when people should rotate.

☐ **Preparation**

Participants must have basic enterprise Canvas training and understand the concept of creating a team business model.

☐ **Procedure**

1. Explain that participants are going to create a business model for their team. Divide the group into sub-teams with two or three members each (groups of four or more members tend to be less effective). You can create the teams at random or decide beforehand who should work with whom.

2. Ask sub-teams to diagram the overall team business model. Put a time limit on this work (15 to 30 minutes is a good range) and stick to the schedule (projecting a timer helps people stay on track). Each sub-team should do this independently without referring to others' work.

3. At the end of this timed session, give the following instruction: "First, assign one of your members to be the 'explainer' of your team model. The others will be 'visitors.' Then, we will do a 'jigsaw' in timed six-minute segments. When you hear the bell, the explainer of your team business model will remain by your Canvas, while the visitors move clockwise to the next group's Canvas. There, they will hear an explanation of that group's interpretation of the team business model, and ask questions. You will have six minutes to do this, so be brisk! Visitors are free to use sticky notes to comment on business models. When you hear the bell again, rotate again to the next group's Canvas, listen to that explanation and ask questions. We will do this until all visitors have seen all the different versions of our team business model. The explainers will stay with their Canvases and not move around the room."

4. Execute the timed rotations. If you have four groups, for example, you will need to have people rotate four times. If they choose to do so, explainers can modify their models on the spot in response to visitor feedback.

5. Have the visitors return to their original positions and discuss what they learned from their colleagues and the alternative team models. They should then revise or refine their team business model to reflect their insights or deeper understanding.

6. Now everyone in the room understands several versions of a team model. You could conduct a general discussion, have each sub-team present their (revised) model, or use another traditional approach to agreeing on the final model. But consider using an alternative methodology such as dotmocracy (described on the next page) to collectively agree on a team model.

Dotmocracy: A Simple Way to Share Decision Making

Dotmocracy is a simple way to share decision making. It democratizes the process of prioritizing or selecting between multiple alternative proposals, ideas, or actions. It is sometimes called *dot voting*, or *voting with dots*.[1]

☐ **Purpose**

Achieve consensus in a group by "voting" rather than debating. The process helps avoid problems with traditional discussions, such as giving excessive weight to the opinions of the most confident speakers, or creating a "bandwagon effect" whereby participants tend to agree with a prevailing view or with the group's dominant personality or highest-ranking leader.

☐ **Method**

Create a visual "ballot" listing all options under consideration. Participants vote by placing sticky notes or dots next to their preferred options. The result is a clear visual depiction of the options most preferred by the group as a whole.

☐ **Number of Participants**

At least three participants are needed. The exercise can be conducted with many more people, though tallying the votes may take more time.

☐ **Time Needed**

Anywhere from five minutes to an hour or more. The voting and tallying can usually be quickly completed, depending on the number of participants. Most of the time is needed to generate, present, and discuss options prior to voting.

☐ **Materials and Tools Needed**

1) Canvases, flipchart(s), a whiteboard, or large self-stick sheets to place on a wall (this description assumes you have just completed the Jigsaw Exercise with Canvases, described on the previous page), and
2) sticky dots or notes, at least five per participant.

☐ How to Vote

First, your group needs options to vote on. If you have just completed the Jigsaw Exercise, you will have a number of team of business model Canvases spread around the room. Explain that participants are going to "vote" for the five building block elements they feel are most important to the team business model. Each participant will get five votes. Participants can cast more than one vote per building block element if they feel strongly about a certain choice, but they must cast votes in at least three different building blocks (modify this rule as you see fit).

Pass out five sticky dots to each participant. Tell them that at your signal, they are to walk freely around the room and place dots next to their most-preferred building block elements, on any of the Canvases (having everyone vote at once keeps participant preferences more or less anonymous).

☐ How to Tally

Ask two participants to count the votes (asking junior or shy participants to do this can help distribute participation). Meanwhile, the rest of the group can take a break or go to lunch. Important note: the counters should first group similar building block elements and write a single descriptor for each cluster. If the Customer building block includes "finance," "accounting," and "finance people," for example, the counters might create a single descriptor labeled "internal finance" and assign it three votes. If the dots are highly concentrated, the results may be immediately obvious, and the counting eliminated or quickly accomplished without taking a break. Note: Five votes per participant seems to work well, but this is not a hard and fast rule.

☐ The Winner(s)

Create a new team Canvas by starting with the top five "winning" building block elements. The rest of the elements can be added based on greatest number of votes received. Congratulations! You have collectively defined your team business model. Even if some participants disagree with the results, they are far more likely to support the group's choices—because they were consulted on the decision and had an equal say in the outcome.

5. Discuss, Decide, Do

Now it is time to discuss the implications of your business model insights and agree on what to do. Look back on the actions described in previous chapter case studies. Those teams looked for and found things to:

- Fix or improve
- Eliminate (do less)
- Reinforce (do more)
- Realign
- Take advantage of

Fast-Forward the Movie helps your team move from agreeing on implications to agreeing on actions.

Fast-Forward the Movie

This handy, easy-to-use exercise helps people become aware of the context surrounding new work assignments, shifts in team activity, personal transitions, or just about any other work-to-be-done. The idea is to elicit insights before the work begins by "fast-forwarding the movie of the work." You can use it anytime without preparation. Here is how:

1. Ask the team to think of the upcoming work as a movie (have them title the movie if they like) Say, "Fast-forward the movie of this project. What does it looks like at the end?" (if you prefer, you can break into small groups that work on this separately). You can ask people to create titles, storyboards, or even a cast of characters for their "movie" if you like. Make suggestions such as, "What unexpected things happened along the way? Describe the biggest challenges and how they were overcome. What was the most exciting scene? Who were the actors? Is your movie a comedy? A tragedy? An adventure story?"

2. Have each group present their movie. As prompts, you could ask people to describe scenes at specific times in the future. With a larger or more mixed group, you could ask people to briefly describe the ending or "scenes" on index cards, then have them trade cards, read each other's notes, then read several aloud. This helps distribute participation.

3. Discuss responses. Give equal weight to rational and intuitive insights. Ask the group to suggest how they might use the insights to make the upcoming work more successful.

☐ **Variation 1**

Divide the team into two groups. One group fast-forwards a "tragic ending" of the movie, describing where, when, and why disaster struck. The other group fast-forwards a "happy ending" version of the movie, describing opportunities, actions, and decisions that resulted in success. Have each group present its version of the movie. Compare the two versions, then discuss implications with the entire group.

With long-term projects, you may want to do this exercise again mid-way. Hint: Save the descriptions of different versions of the movie. After the work is complete, "replay" them during your debriefing.

☐ **Variation 2**

Fast-Forward the Movie can be used with individuals, too. If a team member is struggling with a decision to move from a technical to a leadership role, for example, you might ask them to "Fast-forward the movie of your life as a manager. How are you spending most of your time? Describe how things are different for you now as a manager. What has changed?"

A Final Offer

Whether you lead formally or informally, facility with business models will give you the ability to help people work more effectively: as individuals, in teams, and as contributors to a greater enterprise. So stop thinking about it—go out and give it a try! Experiment. And enjoy yourself in the process.

Finally, we are keen to hear the lessons you learn, whether they come from failure or success. Contact us at tim@BusinessModelsForTeams.com or at bruce@BusinessModelsForTeams.com. And if the spirit moves you, please join us at BusinessModelsForTeams.com, where you can sign up to receive all the tools described in the book, free of charge.

Tim Clark

Bruce Hazen

Portland, Oregon
November 2016

Special Contributors

In addition to the online collaboration, a subset of our co-creator group met in person in Amsterdam for a full day to shape and refine the book. We are grateful to this special team of contributors, especially for testing and critiquing the book's methods and techniques.

Arnulv Rudland
Atos Consulting

Birgitte Alstrøm
ValueGrower

Daniel Weiss
Brickme.org

Dennis Daems
EIFFEL

Edmund Komar
people.innovation.partners

Dr. Frederic Caufrier
Three Parallel Rivers

Jos Meijer
In Good Company

Dr. Jutta Hastenrath
Hastenrath.de

Luigi Centenaro
BigName.it

Marijn Mulders
Tolo Branca

Mercedes Hoss
Off-Time GmbH

Mikko Mannila
Stattys

Nicolas de Vicq
Mindstep.TV

Neil McGregor
Human Synergistics New Zealand

Reiner Walter
Geschäftsmodell-Coach

Renate Bouwman
De Droombaanfabriek

Dr. Thomas Becker
Thomas Becker, btc

Tim & Bruce
BusinessModelsForTeams.com

243

Capturing Practical Inspiration from a Global Community

Meaningful discussions of teamwork cannot happen in theory bubbles or organizational vacuums. Because of this, the authors and the community were dedicated to sharing practical approaches in a deeply actionable book.

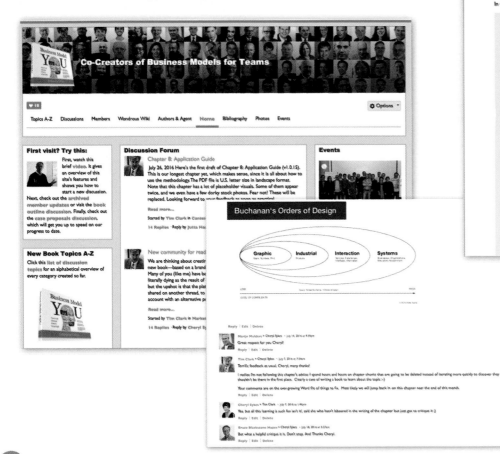

The online community that created *Business Models for Teams* harnessed a global desire for better teamwork. Distributed intelligence brought forth diverse working examples. Ideas and text drafts were tested concurrently.

Writing meant discarding a lot of material and saying just enough to help readers discover how their organizations work—and how people fit in.

Off-line testing and discussion prioritized and refined the best ideas.

From the many things that could be said, we distilled the key things that must be said about business models for teams.

Creator Biographies

Dr. Timothy Clark, Author

Tim is a NEXT-certified entrepreneurship trainer, educator, and author who leads the global personal business model movement at BusinessModelYou.com. After selling his six-year-old startup to a NASDAQ-listed entity in a multi-million-dollar transaction, he completed doctoral research in international business model portability and authored or edited five books on entrepreneurship, business models, and personal development, including the international bestsellers *Business Model You* and *Business Model Generation,* which together have sold more than one million copies in 30 languages.

Previously Tim served as a consultant and researcher for clients such as Amazon.com, Bertelsmann Financial Services, Intel, and PeopleSoft. For six years he authored the monthly Japan Entrepreneur Report and Japan Internet Report newsletters, and wrote the first-ever syndicated English-language research reports covering Japan's Web and Internet-enabled mobile telephone sectors. A Stanford University graduate, he holds master's and doctorate degrees in business administration and has served as a professor at the University of Tsukuba and as Senior Fellow for Tokyo-based venture-capital firm Sunbridge.

Bruce Blackstone Hazen, M.S., Co-Author

Bruce is a career and management consultant who has guided leaders and their followers to personally tailored answers to The Three Career Questions for over 18 years. As a speaker, trainer, and consultant, his mission is clear: reduce workplace suffering, increase career satisfaction, give clients a bigger theory of the game, and prevent them from spending their careers finding "one-job-in-a-row." He earned undergraduate and master's degrees in Industrial and Labor Relations and Clinical Psychology from Cornell University and San Jose State University, respectively, and for 25 years served in both human resource and line management positions in the technology, healthcare, and professional service sectors.

Bruce is the President of Three Questions Consulting and the author of *Answering The Three Career Questions: Your Lifetime Career Management System.* He co-authored the career coaching chapter in *The Complete Handbook of Coaching* and was a contributing co-author to *Business Model You.*

Keiko Onodera, Designer

A Tokyo native, Keiko graduated from the Kuwsawa Design School. While a student, she worked at design studio and created the official Takigawa Beauty College logo, which is still in use today. Following graduation, she was hired as a packaging designer by foodmaker Yukijirushi's R&D center, the largest such research group in Japan, where she was granted patents for her innovative designs. Next, she joined a team of more than 100 creatives at global cosmetics giant Shiseido, where she designed promotional products and packaging.

Keiko moved to the United States in 1991 and worked with Honolulu-based visual design firm UCI, focusing on graphics and packaging, while serving as a freelance graphic designer for magazines and other publications. She then co-founded an online market research and customer acquisition services consultancy, where she designed Japanese language Web sites and online marketing programs for clients such as Amazon.com, JCPenney, and Neiman Marcus. Today she works as an independent designer.

Notes

Chapter 1

1. Author's personal experience in San Jose, California.

2. Daniel Pink's *Drive* offers a comprehensive discussion of human motivation research that posits purpose, autonomy, and mastery as three key workplace motivators. We have added relatedness, which is widely accepted in the social sciences literature as another key motivator.

3. Lencioni, Patrick. *The Five Dysfunctions of a Team* (Jossey-Bass, 2002).

4. Wilson, Edward O. *The Meaning of Human Existence* (LiveRight Publishing Corporation, 2014).

5. Hersey, P., and Blanchard, K. H. *Life Cycle Theory of Leadership* (Training and Development Journal 23 (5): 26–34. 1969).

6. Blanchard, K. H. *The One Minute Manager.* See also the Center for Creative Leadership (http://www.ccl .org/).

7. Marciano, Paul. *Carrots and Sticks Don't Work: Build a Culture of Employee Engagement with the Principles of RESPECT*™ (McGraw-Hill, 2010).

8. Formal systems thinking is too difficult for most people and therefore impractical for many leaders. See Donella Meadows's *Thinking in Systems: A Primer* as an excellent, non-specialist introduction to systems thinking.

9. We define third objects as physical artifacts that, when used in a structured but somewhat gamelike way, significantly surpass discussion in their capacity to deepen relationships between people and their understanding of complex subjects. The word "third" refers both to 1) something external to those present, and 2) an additional physical dimension that moves understanding beyond linear, word-based interactions.

10. Kristiansen, Per, and Rasmussen, Robert. *Building a Better Business Using the LEGO® Serious Play® Method* (Wiley, 2014).

11. Osterwalder, Alexander, Pigneur, Yves, et al. *Value Proposition Design* (Wiley, 2014).

Chapter 2

1. Owen, David. *Copies in Seconds: Chester Carlson and the Birth of the Xerox Machine* (Simon & Schuster, 2004), 220.

2. Chesbrough, Henry, and Rosenblum, Richard S. *The Role of the Business Model in Capturing Value from Innovation: Evidence from Xerox Corporation's Technology Spinoff Companies* (Harvard Business School).

3. *Copies in Seconds*, 278.

4. Intense competition from Japanese copier manufacturers was also a critical factor. See Charles D. Ellis's *Joe Wilson and the Creation of Xerox* (Wiley, 2006).

5. NASDAQ calculation as of April 27, 2016.

6. Alexander Osterwalder and Yves Pigneur define business model this way: *a business model describes the rationale of how an organization creates, delivers, and captures value* (from *Business Model Generation*, Wiley, 2010). We find it more intuitive to think of value as being "captured" by Customers rather than by the organization that creates and delivers it.

7. In *Business Model Generation*, Channels encompass all five phases of the marketing process. We find it more intuitive to think of Channels encompassing the first four marketing phases that lead to prospects being converted to Customers. After prospects become Customers, the organization communicates with them via the Customer Relationships building block.

8. Visit Strategyzer.com for tools that enable either local or cloud-based creation of digitized Business Model Canvases and cost calculations.

9. The Business Model Canvas was invented by Alexander Osterwalder and Yves Pigneur and can be obtained free of charge at Strategyzer.com.

Chapter 3

1. Lencioni, Patrick. *The Three Signs of a Miserable Job* (Jossey-Bass, 2007).

2. Search "Clayton Christensen" and "jobs to be done" for more on this concept. For a comprehensive dis-

cussion of pains and gains, see Alexander Oster-walder and Yves Pigneur's *Value Proposition Design* (Wiley, 2014).

Chapter 4

1. If you have not yet drawn your own personal business model, see author Tim Clark's *Business Model You* (Wiley, 2012) or visit CommunityBusinessModelYou.com to view free, step-by-step "how-to" videos.

2. Personal Value Proposition is described as "Value Provided" in *Business Model You.* The two terms are interchangeable. "Value Provided" is used to denote someone currently working and already delivering Value, as opposed to "Value Proposition," which implies the person is seeking new Customers by proposing to deliver a certain Value.

3. Search "Clayton Christensen" and "jobs-to-be-done" for more on this concept.

4. Frederic Laloux discusses the "whole self" idea in *Reinventing Organizations: A Guide to Creating Organizations Inspired by the Next Stage of Human Consciousness* (Nelson Parker, 2014).

5. Paraphrased quote attributed to Holocracy One co-founder Tom Thomison.

6. Lencioni, Patrick. *The Truth About Employee Engagement* (Jossey-Bass, 2015).

7. www.reachcc.com/.

Chapter 5

1. See Daniel Pink's *Drive,* a comprehensive discussion of human motivation research that posits purpose, autonomy, and mastery as three key workplace motivators. We have added relatedness, a key motivator under Self-Determination Theory.

2. See co-author Bruce Hazen's *Answering the Three Career Questions* (Three Questions Consulting, 2014) for a comprehensive discussion of career collaboration.

3. See *Answering the Three Career Questions* for a comprehensive discussion of the Three Questions.

4. LinkedIn Exit Survey, 2014.

5. Towers Watson Global Workforce Study, 2014.

6. See JobCrafting.org.

Chapter 6

1. The Golden Circle was created by Simon Sinek and described in *Start With Why* (Random House, 2008).

2. Lencioni, Patrick. *The Truth About Employee Engagement* (Jossey-Bass, 2015).

3. This exercise is described as "Low-Tech Social Network" in Dave Gray's *Gamestorming* (O'Reilly, 2010).

4. Exercise adapted from Sinek, *Start With Why.*

5. Ibid.

Chapter 7

1. This story is based on an author engagement. Names have been changed for privacy. Dialogue and some events have been fictionalized for teaching purposes. Photographs are of the actual workplace.

Chapter 8

1. Refer to Tim Clark's *Business Model You* (Wiley, 2012) or visit BusinessModelYou.com.

2. Covey, Stephen. *The 7 Habits of Highly Effective People* (Free Press, 1990).

3. Blanchard, Ken. *Mastering the Art of Change* (Training Journal, January 2010).

4. Marciano, Paul. *Carrots and Sticks Don't Work: Build a Culture of Employee Engagement with the Principles of RESPECT™* (McGraw-Hill, 2010).

5. Empathy Maps are described in in Gray, David, et al. *Gamestorming* (O'Reilly, 2010).

Chapter 9

1. Dotmocracy is described in in Gray, David, et al. *Gamestorming* (O'Reilly, 2010).

Books and Articles You May Find Useful

Argyris, Chris. *Integrating the Individual and the Organization* (Transaction Publishers, 1990)

Beck, Don Edward, and Cowan, Christopher C. *Spiral Dynamics: Mastering Values, Leadership, and Change* (Blackwell Publishing, 1996, 2006)

Berger, Jennifer Garvey, and Johnston, Keith. *Simple Habits for Complex Times: Powerful Practices for Leaders* (Stanford University Press, 2015)

Buxton, Bill. *Sketching User Experiences: Getting the Design Right and the Right Design* (Elsevier, 2007)

Cappelli, Peter. *Why Good People Can't Get Jobs: The Skills Gap and What Companies Can Do About It* (Wharton Digital Press, 2012)

Chandler, M. Tamra. *How Performance Management is Killing Performance—and What to Do About It* (Barrett Koehler Publishers, Inc., 2016)

Clark, Tim, Osterwalder, Alexander, and Pigneur, Yves. *Business Model You* (Wiley, 2012)

Eoyang, Glenda, and Holladay, Royce J. *Adaptive Action: Leveraging Uncertainty in Your Organization* (Stanford Business Books, 2013)

Fuller, R. Buckminster. *Operating Manual for Spaceship Earth* (Lars Müller Publishers, 2008)

Getz, Issac. *Liberating Leadership: How the Initiative-Freeing Radical Organizational Form Has Been Successfully Adopted* (California Management Review, 2009 Vol. 51, No. 4)

Gray, David, et al. *Gamestorming* (O'Reilly, 2010)

Hamel, Gary. *What Matters Now* (Jossey-Bass, 2012)

Haudan, Jim. *The Art of Engagement: Bridging the Gap Between People and Possibilities* (McGraw-Hill, 2008)

Hazen, Bruce. *Answering the Three Career Questions* (Three Questions Consulting, 2014)

Hsieh, Tony. *Delivering Happiness: A Path to Profits, Passion, and Purpose* (Grand Central Publishing, 2010)

Hock, Dee. *One From Many: VISA and the Rise of the Chaordic Organization* (Barrett Koehler Publications, Inc., 2005)

Kaye, Beverly, and Giulioni, Julie Winkle. *Help Them Grow or Watch Them Go: Career Conversations Employees Want* (Barrett-Koehler Publications, 2012)

Kersten, E.L. *The Art of Demotivation—A Visionary Guide for Transforming Your Company's Least Valuable Asset: Your Employees* (Despair, Inc., 2005)

Kolko, Jon. *Design Thinking Comes of Age* (Harvard Business Review, September 2015)

Krames, Jeffrey. *Lead With Humility: 12 Leadership Lessons from Pope Francis* (American Management Association, 2015)

Kristiansen, Per, and Rasmussen, Robert. *Building a Better Business Using the Lego® Serious Play® Method* (Wiley, 2014)

Kruse, Kevin. *Employee Engagement for Everyone* (Center for Wholehearted Leadership, 2013)

Labovitz, George, and Rosansky, Victor. *The Power of Alignment: How Great Companies Stay Centered and Accomplish Extraordinary Things* (McGraw-Hill, 1997)

Labovitz, George, and Rosansky, Victor. *Rapid Realignment: How to Quickly Integrate People, Processes, and Strategy for Unbeatable Performance* (McGraw-Hill, 2012)

Laloux, Frederic. *Reinventing Organizations: A Guide to Creating Organizations Inspired by the Next Stage of Human Consciousness* (Nelson Parker, 2014)

Lencioni, Patrick. *The Five Dysfunctions of a Team* (Jossey-Bass, 2002)

Lencioni, Patrick. *The Truth About Employee Engagement* (Jossey-Bass, 2015)

Marciano, Paul. *Carrots and Sticks Don't Work: Build a Culture of Employee Engagement with the Principles of RESPECT™* (McGraw-Hill, 2010)

Marquet, L. David. *Turn the Ship Around! A True Story of Turning Followers into Leaders* (Portfolio/Penguin, 2012)

Maturana, Humberto R., and Varela, Francisco J. *The Tree of Knowledge: The Biological Roots of Human Understanding* (Shambhala, 1987)

Mayer, Roger C., Davis, James H., and Schoorman, F. David. *An Integrative Model of Organizational Trust* (The Academy of Management Review, Vol. 20, No. 3, July 1995)

Maylett, Tracy, and Warner, Paul. *MAGIC: Five Keys to Unlock the Power of Employee Engagement* (Greenleaf, 2014)

McCarthy, Robert. *Navigating with Trust* (Rockbench, 2012)

Meadows, Donella. *Thinking in Systems: A Primer* (Chelsea Green Publishing, 2008)

Osterwalder, Alexander, and Pigneur, Yves. *Business Model Generation* (Wiley, 2010)

Osterwalder, Alexander, and Pigneur, Yves, et al. *Value Proposition Design* (Wiley, 2014)

Pink, Daniel. *Drive* (Riverhead Books, 2011)

Semler, Ricardo. *Maverick: The Success Story Behind the World's Most Unusual Workplace* (Grand Central Publishing, 1993)

Senge, Peter. *The Fifth Discipline Field Book* (Bantam Doubleday Dell Publishing Group, Inc., 1994)

Simon, Hermann. *Hidden Champions of the 21st Century: Success Strategies of Unknown World Market Leaders* (Springer, 2009)

Sinek, Simon. *Start With Why: How Great Leaders Inspire Everyone to Take Action* (Portfolio, 2011)

Wilson, Edward O. *The Meaning of Human Existence* (LiveRight Publishing Corporation, 2014)

Wlodkowski, Raymond J. *Enhancing Adult Motivation to Learn: A Comprehensive Guide for Teaching All Adults* (Jossey-Bass, 2008)

Index

Note: Page numbers in *italics* refer to illustrations, charts, or graphs.

We have pre-spilled coffee here so you will not hesitate to write or doodle on these pages.

PORTFOLIO / PENGUIN
An imprint of Penguin Random House LLC
375 Hudson Street
New York, New York 10014
penguin.com

Most Portfolio books are available at a discount when purchased in quantity for sales promotions or corporate use. Special editions, which include personalized covers, excerpts, and corporate imprints, can be created when purchased in large quantities. For more information, please call (212) 572-2232 or e-mail specialmarkets@penguinrandomhouse.com. Your local bookstore can also assist with discounted bulk purchases using the Penguin Random House corporate Business-to-Business program. For assistance in locating a participating retailer, e-mail B2B@penguinrandomhouse.com.

LIBRARY OF CONGRESS CATALOGING-IN-PUBLICATION DATA

Names: Clark, Tim, 1956- author. | Hazen, Bruce, author.
Title: Business models for teams : see how your organization really works and how each person fits in /
    by Tim Clark and Bruce Hazen, in collaboration with 225 contributors from 39 countries ;
    designed by Keiko Onodera.
Description: New York : Portfolio/Penguin, [2017]
Identifiers: LCCN 2016058687 (print) | LCCN 2017016392 (ebook) | ISBN 9780735213470 (ebook) |
    ISBN 9780735213357 (pbk.)
Subjects: LCSH: Organizational effectiveness. | Teams in the workplace. | Management.
Classification: LCC HD58.9 (ebook) | LCC HD58.9 .C624 2017 (print) | DDC 658.4/022—dc23
LC record available at https://lccn.loc.gov/2016058687

Printed in the United States of America
10 9 8 7 6 5 4 3 2 1

Set in Whitney
Designed by Keiko Onodera

33614080225682

While the author has made every effort to provide accurate Internet addresses and other contact information at the time of publication, neither the publisher nor the author assumes any responsibility for errors or for changes that occur after publication. Further, the publisher does not have any control over and does not assume any responsibility for author or third-party Web sites or their content.

This publication is designed to provide accurate and authoritative information in regard to the subject matter covered. It is sold with the understanding that the publisher is not engaged in rendering legal, accounting, or other professional services. If you require legal advice or other expert assistance, you should seek the services of a competent professional.